BFI Film Classics

The BFI Film Classics series introduces, interprets and celebrates landmarks of world cinema. Each volume offers an argument for the film's 'classic' status, together with discussion of its production and reception history, its place within a genre or national cinema, an account of its technical and aesthetic importance, and in many cases, the author's personal response to the film.

For a full list of titles in the series, please visit https://www.bloomsbury.com/uk/series/bfi-film-classics/

On 12 January 1953, the Toulouse Cine Club attempted an experiment when showing *Murder, My Sweet* a few weeks before the distribution rights lapsed. This involved finding out whether this film would create in the viewer that state of tension and malaise that the critics had been unanimous in describing seven years before. The experiment was negative. Marlowe's third blackout, which at the time had elicited a genuine feeling of anguish, provoked a general outburst of laughter.

Raymond Borde and Étienne Chaumeton,
A Panorama of American Film Noir 1941–1953

The Big Lebowski

J. M. Tyree &
Ben Walters

THE BRITISH FILM INSTITUTE
Bloomsbury Publishing Plc
50 Bedford Square, London, WC1B 3DP, UK
1385 Broadway, New York, NY 10018, USA

BLOOMSBURY is a trademark of Bloomsbury Publishing Plc

First published in 2007 by the British Film Institute
This edition first published in 2020 by Bloomsbury on behalf of the
British Film Institute
21 Stephen Street, London W1T 1LN
www.bfi.org.uk

The BFI is the lead organisation for film in the UK and the distributor of Lottery funds
for film. Our mission is to ensure that film is central to our cultural life, in particular
by supporting and nurturing the next generation of filmmakers and audiences. We serve
a public role which covers the cultural, creative and economic aspects of film in the UK.

Cover artwork © Max Loeffler
Series cover design: Louise Dugdale
Series text design: ketchup/SE14
Images from *The Big Lebowski* © 1998 Polygram Filmed Entertainment Inc.

A catalogue record for this book is available from the British Library.

A catalog record for this book is available from the Library of Congress.

ISBN: PB: 9781838719609
        ePDF: 9781838719586
        ePUB: 9781838719593

Series: BFI Film Classics

Typeset by Newgen KnowledgeWorks Pvt. Ltd., Chennai, India
Printed and bound in India

To find out more about our authors and books visit
www.bloomsbury.com and sign up for our newsletters.

Contents

Foreword to the 2020 Edition

Since we wrote this book in 2007, *The Big Lebowski*'s status has grown from cult to classic, featuring on most 'best-ever comedy' (if not 'best-ever movie') lists and feeding ever-growing cottage industries of devoted fandom and academic analysis. The movie now has broad enough mainstream recognition for Jeff Bridges to play the Dude in a Super Bowl commercial and for a portly, laid-back incarnation of a Marvel superhero to be widely known as 'Lebowski Thor'. The word 'dude' slipped into Boris Johnson's victory speech during his installation as British prime minister in July 2019. We were even asked to write about the film for the United States Library of Congress, which feels pretty canonical.

And the Coens themselves have been elevated from indie-arthouse darlings to bona fide Best Picture Oscar-winning industry big shots. This has happened without the bastardization of their distinctive sensibility, which both affirms their self-determined savvy and reminds us how imbricated that sensibility has always been with classical Hollywood terms.

Our working theory of the film – that it is really fucking funny – hasn't changed. And even if *The Big Lebowski* is now old enough to buy itself a White Russian, its richly layered text continues to yield new delights. We noticed only recently, for instance, how redolent the nihilists' bizarre ransom delivery instructions are of a similarly complex set-up in Akira Kurosawa's *High & Low* (1963), in which the cash is thrown from a moving train. Intentional or not, this resonance might be a droll way of indicating that the nihilists went to art school and got their ideas about how to stage a kidnapping from a vaguely remembered undergrad survey course on world cinema.

We're happy that the past decade has been kind to the Coens and *Lebowski*. As admirers of the Dude's nuanced, laconic, violence-averse and humane worldview, however, we're dismayed that the same period has seen an upswing in polarization, conflict, simplification and othering. Big Lebowskis, not Dudes, stalk the land: sexist, racist, rich old white men fixed on rapacious and regressive notions of 'achievement'; phony goldbrickers; human paraquats oozing toxic masculinity. It might even feel as if the revolution really is over and – condolences! – the bums lost.

Today, some of the movie's absurdities take on a curious poignancy. Its celebration of promiscuous plurality feels even more valuable. The Dude's iconic status, including among many people younger than the movie itself, suggests an appetite for a more easeful, open and present-minded way of living – post-ambition cosplay, perhaps, for a time of fraught precarity. And, for all its bombast, the Dude's friendship with Walter only grows more affecting and instructive thanks to its unstated premises of connection across difference, tolerance of shortcomings, acceptance of accountability and forgiveness of harm.

Lebowski joins rare company in cinema history, a comedy that's also a classic. Like other great comedies, it lives on not through pretension to universalism or impeccable anticipation of the norms and values of future generations but rather through its idiosyncrasy and blatant unacceptability in polite company. Somewhat in the manner of Chaplin's jokes about starvation and cannibalism in *The Gold Rush* (1924), Lubitsch's jaunty mockery of fascist war crimes in *To Be or Not to Be* (1942) or Kubrick's slapstick vision of nuclear armageddon in *Dr Strangelove* (1964), the Coens cartoonishly engage everything from police brutality and the tenets of National Socialism to sex-offender registers and the nuances of preferred nomenclatures related to ethnicity and disability. All without melodrama, hand-wringing or losing a beat – or, crucially, losing sight of each and every character's humanity.

If the film continues to work its magic for future audiences (one never knows), this humane consideration might be the reason. There is something cosmic about the view of a sometimes redeemable and largely lovable world that is nevertheless filled to the gills with human folly. Perhaps we're just rambling again, or blathering about a bygone era filled with our own youthful enthusiasm for a great popular comedy, but *The Big Lebowski* still makes us laugh to beat the band. We take comfort in that.

July 2019

Whence 'Lebowski'?

While writing this book in 2007, we wondered how the Coen brothers came up with the name Jeffrey Lebowski but couldn't find any information. In 2018, around the release of *The Ballad of Buster Scruggs*, Ben interviewed the Coens and asked them. Here's what they said:

ETHAN	A neighbour. Childhood, uh—
JOEL	It's a friend of— Yeah, it was a neighbour in the little suburb we grew up in.
ETHAN	Didn't Jeff Lebowski— Isn't he, like, attorney general of the state or something? He had some prominence. [Jeff Lebowski became General Counsel in the Minnesota Department of Labor and Industry.]
JOEL	Our sister, her best friend was Bonnie Lebowski.
ETHAN	And her brother was Jeff, right? It was Jeff?
JOEL	Oh, I think so. I don't know if it was her brother. I think it was a relative. I'm not sure. Anyway, yeah. It comes from there.
ETHAN	We once complimented Paul Schrader on the end of *Taxi Driver*. He [Robert De Niro] gets the note from the parents to Jodie Foster and it's signed 'Burt and Ivy Steensma' and we complimented him on the name and he said, 'Childhood friends.'

JOEL   My mother, when she was still alive, whenever she— would beg us
          to stop using the names of neighbours, in our movies, and friends
          of theirs when we were growing up. She would— 'Please, would
          you stop using—?' 'Cause we did do that constantly. Mrs Samsky
          [used in *A Serious Man*] was our next-door neighbour when we
          were growing up.

ETHAN   The studio head in *Barton Fink* was our rabbi, Jack Lipnick. Well,
          actually, Jerry Lipnick.

Acknowledgements

Collaborative writing sharpened our ideas and doubled our luck in finding connections, tracking down sources and catching at least some of our errors. It also gave us an appreciation for the working methods of artists who, like the Coens but unlike most critics, prefer not to work alone. This book benefitted from dozens of conversations with friends, family and fans: *The Big Lebowski* is a movie that makes people happy to talk. In addition, the following people have our thanks for their contributions to this study: Geoff Andrew, Rebecca Barden, Tom Cabot, Sophia Contento, Jeffrey Alan Fiskin, Lee Grieveson, Hillary Harrison, Kyle Krueger, Monica King, Morgan Meis, Chris, Lois, Joanna & Emily Mitchell, Fabio Periera, Charlie Plotkin & Wendy Brandchaft, Will Russell, Scott Shuffitt, David, Jessica & Oliver Walters and Sarah Watt.

Introduction

In July 2002, two bored vendors at the Derby City Tattoo Expo in Louisville, Kentucky, began quoting lines from *The Big Lebowski* to entertain themselves. Other workers nearby joined in with surprising enthusiasm and the pair, Will Russell and Scott Shuffitt, hatched the idea of a *Lebowski* convention. Three months later, they hired Louisville's cheapest bowling alley – which, being run by Baptists, didn't allow drinking or swearing, two of the film's primary pleasures – and hoped twenty or thirty friends would show up to cover the costs of their First Annual Big Lebowski What-Have-You Fest. More than 150 people showed, from as far afield as Arizona and New York State. Some of them even came in fancy dress, as characters from the film. They had fun.

Since then, thousands of 'Achievers' have travelled from across the US and the world to attend over a dozen of Russell and Shuffitt's 'Lebowski Fests' in Louisville, Las Vegas, New York, Austin and Los Angeles. Other Fests have been held around the globe. The costume

Are You A Lebowski Achiever? Thousands answered yes

thing really took off, quickly spreading from the main characters to the minor ones, then to people mentioned only in passing, props and materialisations of figures of speech: Achievers came as the Dude's landlord in his vine-wreathed dance leotard; Mrs Jamtoss, the teacher whose name appears for a split second on the piece of homework left by a teenage joyrider in the Dude's car; the queen in her damned undies (mentioned aphoristically by the narrator); a Creedence Clearwater Revival tape; a severed toe. The Fests have boasted appearances from Jeff Dowd (the main real-life model for the Dude), Peter Stormare (who played Uli the nihilist) and David Huddleston (the Big Lebowski), and Jeff Bridges brought the house down in L.A. by performing the Dude's signature tune, 'The Man in Me'. Yet the actors who played Jesus Quintana's bowling partner, the dream-sequence Saddam and the Ralph's supermarket checkout girl have been rapturously received too, despite appearing on screen for mere seconds. You can buy copies of the Dude's poster of Nixon bowling, or bumper stickers emblazoned with key lines from the script ('This aggression will not stand, man'; 'The bums will always lose'). You

'The Dudes' at the 5th Annual Lebowski Fest in Louisville, Kentucky (30 Sept, 2006) (Picture: Hillary Harrison)

can enter ringer-tossing and marmot-flinging contests. Neighbouring convenience stores have doubled their nightly income following runs on dairy products to make White Russians.[1]

Since every last scrap of dialogue from the film is now somebody's inside joke – oat sodas! what-have-you! – *The Big Lebowski* is now basically a slacker's bible, to be quoted more or less religiously. In fact, the website Dudeism.com elevates the Dude to the status of religious guru, while the Lebowski Fest forums contain photos of Achievers holding up quasi-biblical signs reading 'Lebowski 7:19' or other chapter-and-verse markers. (These seem to have started as references to Fest dates before taking on a life of their own, with Lebowski signage recorded at locations across the globe: the viewing platform of the Empire State Building, Tiananmen Square, the deserts of Chile, etc.) Interest in the film is not restricted to worshipful quotation. The 2006 Louisville Fest included a symposium in which professional academics presented such papers as 'Lebowski/Mnemosyne: Cultural Memory, Cultural Authority, and Forgetfulness', 'Obscene Enjoyment and the Port Huron Statement' and 'Don't Fuck with the Jesus: *The Big Lebowski*, Ritual and (Imposed) Narratives of the Self'.[2] In the Fests' online forums you can find discussions of whether the Dude is truly 'a hero' and fan-fiction treatments for possible sequels, as well as notes on Walter's occupational status and details of a real-life pederast called Jesus Quintana. Elsewhere on the internet you can find an 'official' website of The Little Lebowski Urban Achievers, with artwork and a page of links to Ralph's, the City of Malibu and the American Pomeranian Club.[3]

So how has a film that slipped beneath the waves critically and commercially on its first release in 1998 attained such a devoted following? An attempt to describe its plot offers little to go on. The setting is Los Angeles, 1990. As Iraqi forces invade Kuwait, middle-aged Venice Beach slacker, druggie, bowling aficionado and 1960s throwback Jeffrey Lebowski – known simply as 'the Dude' – encounters unchecked aggression on a more intimate scale. His name has been confused with that of a local grandee whose young trophy wife has run up a sizeable debt to a Malibu pornography king. Goons

attempt to extort the money from the wrong Jeffrey Lebowski, and
wind up urinating on the Dude's most beloved possession, a ratty
little rug that really tied the room together. Seeking compensation
from his namesake, the Dude finds himself improbably recruited as
private investigator in a kidnapping scheme involving the trophy wife
and a nihilist techno band. A slow-witted cowboy narrator, a feminist
artist searching for a sperm donor, a joyriding teenager who is
flunking social studies and the Dude's bowling partner and best
buddy Walter, an oafish and occasionally psychotic gun-toting
Vietnam vet, all get in on the act. But who is actually responsible for
the kidnap – or whether there even *was* a kidnap – becomes less and
less clear... Does this tell us much of anything, except that the film
seems designed with deliberate perversity to thwart Hollywood
conceptions of the brief 'treatment' and the three-second sell?

So let's assume that the appeal of *The Big Lebowski* is not
predominantly narrative. The plot does become clearer on repeated
viewings, but what might be more important is that the film also
becomes funnier, richer and more affecting. *The Big Lebowski* never
lets us down no matter how many times we watch it, something that
can be said of few comedies from this or any other era. The
painstaking yet joyous detail of its execution unquestionably rewards

An improbable recruit

close attention: rather than worrying about who did or didn't do what to whom, the *Lebowski* devotee revels in a world whose extraordinarily fecund absurdities seem to take on a near-universal applicability. 'The Lebowski festival is the tip of the iceberg,' according to Jeff Dowd, who has made something of a second career out of his connection to the film. 'It's remarkable how many people from different walks of life see this movie again and again. Not just potheads. There was a Wall Street guy I met who'd drop a *Lebowski* line into job interviews and if the person didn't pick up on it he wouldn't be hired. I met this commander of a military base. He said they watch the movie down there in the missile silo two or three times a week.'[4] This breadth of appeal seems apt to the atmosphere of warmth and respect that has characterised the Achiever scene from the start. On their website, Russell and Shuffitt recall how the references they shared with others at the Tattoo Expo 'created a sense of bonding and camaraderie never before experienced between complete strangers. It turned what was gearing up to be one sucky weekend into quite a good time.' This is surely an effect of which the Dude would have been proud: if nothing else, his story is a lesson in the boons of good-natured laughter and acceptance.

This is not, however, a perspective that has informed all writing about *The Big Lebowski*. Indeed, critics have not found it easy to write about any of the Coen brothers' films without descending into mere jokiness on one hand or hyper-pretentiousness on the other. Part of the problem is that investigating why something is funny tends not to be funny, or even productive. The Coens have also pre-satirised their critics. In 'Introduction: Lebowski Yes and No', one of many delightful fictional prefaces to their published scripts, they created a pompous pseudo-scholar, Sir Anthony Forte-Bowell, who spoils the fun with his over-zealously academic explanation of the Three Stooges' comedy. 'Even a frame-by-frame analysis of the films', Forte-Bowell writes in his supposedly seminal work *But Is It Funny?*, 'fails to reveal wherein the nature of the humour resides.'[5] The Coens have long delighted in sending up such chaff, in facetious and comically misleading interviews as well as a stable of fake fronts that also includes Forever Young Films (whose 'Mortimer Young' introduces the supposedly 'restored' *Big Lebowski* special edition DVD) and Mike Zoss Productions, which really is their production company but whose website is a farrago of outrageous misinformation. It was only when he was nominated for an Academy Award for his work on *Fargo* that it was widely realised that Roderick Jaynes, regularly credited as the Coens' film editor, did not, in fact, exist. (The hoax was perpetuated in Jaynes's absurd Coen-bashing introductions to the scripts of *Barton Fink/Miller's Crossing* and *The Man Who Wasn't There*, and in Billy Bob Thornton's DVD commentary on the latter film.) Accordingly, some of the best writing on the Coens, like that of William Preston Robertson in *The Big Lebowski: The Making of a Coen Brothers Film*, has been done by insiders who aren't afraid to laugh *at* the film-makers' foibles as well as with them.[6]

When *The Big Lebowski* was released in the UK, one critic suggested that 'comic genius of the Coens' order is for enjoyment rather than analysis'; another commended it to his readers, but with a rider: 'don't discuss it afterwards, because there's nothing to say'.[7] While keen to avoid Forte-Bowellism, we feel that critical engagement with the picture might yet prove worthwhile. The Coens take a wrecking ball to Hollywood movies, and we hope to trace some of the patterns in the rubble – in fact, we insist that *The Big Lebowski* is a film of ideas, a film whose ostensibly ramshackle form turns out to be the perfect vessel for a story whose very subjects are disjunction and miscommunication, the abuse of genre convention and the defiance of received notions of heroism and masculinity. But the last thing we want to do is spoil the fun, to treat the film's humour – unquestionably its most appealing attribute – as merely a vehicle for some 'real' or 'deeper' meaning. If *The Big Lebowski* has anything to teach us, it is the virtue of humble good humour. To dismiss comedy as merely unserious, rather than seriously unserious, is to forget that it is one of the most mysterious, valuable and difficult to achieve of all artistic effects. Laughter itself is the main thing.

1 The Mix-tape Movie

There were two trailers for *The Big Lebowski*. One, aiming to exploit the unexpected success of the Coen brothers' previous film, presented it fairly conventionally as a comic detective movie: 'from the creators of *Fargo* comes the story of a ransom gone wrong'. Audiences attracted by this might have been confused or disappointed by the feature they saw. The other trailer also mentioned *Fargo* (1996), but it didn't make the slightest effort to make sense. Instead it offered a deliberately baffling split-screen barrage of absurdities and *non sequiturs* comprising nine moving images at a time. In one sequence, bowling pins tumble in one frame as Jeff Bridges' head is shoved down a toilet in another and a blond guy peers, perplexed, at a bowling ball in a third. After that, Bridges lies on a wooden floor listening to a Walkman while a fat man in a wheelchair bellows and a starlet type coquettishly lowers her shades. Then Saddam Hussein hands out bowling shoes as Bridges dances,

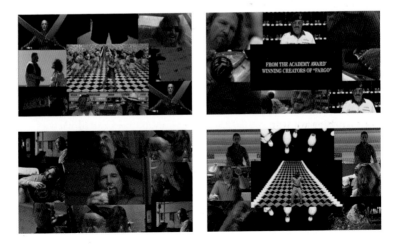

There isn't a literal connection: the absurd incongruities of *The Big Lebowski* trailer

grinning, down a giant chequered staircase and John Turturro dances, very seriously, in a purple shirt. John Goodman attacks a car in one frame while pulling a handgun in another; Bridges enjoys a beverage, milk dripping from his moustache, as he simultaneously thrashes around in a bath; a man in a red catsuit brandishes giant scissors as Bridges talks to a cowboy in a bowling alley and argues with Goodman on a clifftop; a group of bowling-themed Busby Berkeley chorines arrange their bodies into pretty patterns. Huh? It would be a shrewd viewer indeed who came away from all this with the remotest notion of what to expect from this movie, this *Big Lebowski* – other than a lot of bowling. Still, you couldn't say you hadn't been warned.

This second trailer in fact makes a pretty good primer for a film that takes absurd incongruity as its touchstone. A kidnap plot in which no one is really kidnapped, no ransom is handed over and the investigator is submissively bounced from one eccentric encounter to the next, *The Big Lebowski* revels in wanton, riotous variety, apparently for its own sake. A glorious hotch-potch, it might seem to be no more or less than an uncooped menagerie or upturned playbox, an improvised stew of found morsels and flavoursome leftovers, a party with a great soundtrack but no host. Certainly, to get at the heart of the story you've got to pick your way through a bewildering onslaught of ostensibly unconnected goof-offs and curveballs, esoteric dialogue and offbeat locations, off-kilter music and discombobulating genre slippage. But seek and ye shall find: like a cut-and-pasted ransom note, the film's cobbled-together components disguise a real sense of purpose. In marked contrast to one of its primary cinematic sources, Howard Hawks's *The Big Sleep* (1946), *The Big Lebowski* does actually make narrative sense, if you acclimatise to its oddness and pay attention; more than that, it offers what amounts to a lesson in humanity, if you're willing to work through the fiddly squiggles of irony and overlays of vulgar graffiti. What emerges from the tangle is a very funny film about real things and the search for meaning: not just the solution to a mystery, but an ethos by which to navigate a jumbled place in jumbled times. It's just that you've got your work cut out to find it.

The Coen picture

A delight in unexpected collage has always been deeply embedded in the Coens' films, from the absurd yet deadly serious opening voice-over of *Blood Simple* (1984) through *Raising Arizona*'s (1987) banjo rendition of Beethoven's 'Ode to Joy' to the dustbowl shotgun wedding of Homer and the Three Stooges that yielded *O Brother, Where Art Thou?* (2000). 'Even the things that don't go together should seem to clash in an interesting way,' Ethan Coen has said. 'You sort of do it by feel and not with reasons.'[8] In *Raising Arizona*, they cast Goodman and William Forsythe as the troublesome fugitive brothers simply because they looked funny together.

This penchant for absurd juxtaposition applies not just to aspects of individual movies, but to the Coens' entire career. Formally speaking, theirs is an unusually varied oeuvre for film-makers of such critical stature, with works ranging across periods, locations, styles and genres from 1940s Hollywood to contemporary Texas, quasi-realism to the brink of the surreal, screwball comedy to gangland

Opposites attract and worlds collide at Ed and Hi's wedding in *Raising Arizona*, as throughout the Coens' work

politics. They do like crime stories of one kind or another. Consistencies can also be found in their idiosyncratic approach to character, dialogue and certain considerations of technique, such as the predilection for wide-angle lenses and other recurring pet motifs identified by William Preston Robertson.[9] But 'the Coen picture' is a considerably harder beast to taxonomise than, say, 'the Hitchcock picture' or 'the Sirk picture'. You never know what's around the next corner. The Coen *modus operandi* of serial homage bears comparison with that of Billy Wilder. As Richard Schickel notes, Wilder would speak of his 'Lubitsch film', his 'Hitchcock film' and so forth, of trying something 'in a manner he admired'.[10] Wilder, with his chameleon-like adaptability and his style of many styles, was clearly a Coen precursor, making something like *The Man Who Wasn't There* an inevitable collision. Indeed, in that film the Coens attempt a version of the execution scene notoriously cut from *Double Indemnity* (1944).

Yet while the Coens had covered a remarkable amount of ground in the half-dozen films they made before *The Big Lebowski*, each picture had its own highly consistent milieu, from the brass tacks of *Blood Simple* to the semi-cartoonish modernist pastiche of *The Hudsucker Proxy* (1994). *Lebowski*, however, is constantly muddying boundaries and shifting shape; here, for the first time, incongruity becomes the basic key in which a picture is played. In this sense, it could be seen as an archetypal Coen project, an idea of their oeuvre in microcosm: the moving picture as moving target. It is a film of constantly shifting gears – sometimes, the film is literally (and subtly) slowed down then speeded up, as with the shots showing the Dude arriving at Jackie Treehorn's beach party or running along the middle of the highway after his nightmare. Visually too, the movie is relatively chaotic. 'I'm not sure I ever really had a handle on what *Lebowski* should look like,' the Coens' regular cinematographer Roger Deakins has admitted. 'It's such a mix, I don't think it has one style.'[11] Certainly, no other movie has found space for tumbling tumbleweeds, slo-mo bowling, sombre, firelit great-room scenes, geometrically choreographed dance routines *and* VHS porn.

It's equally hard to pin down the film's period. It's set in 1990, a mere six years before its time of production – an awkward gap, long enough to distinguish 'then' from 'now' (check out the size of that mobile phone) but too short for historical perspective or personal nostalgia really to take root. The Coens have hinted that the period was chosen simply so that Walter would have an overseas war to bitch about. But it is altogether apt that the film's period and production book-end the 1990s, the decade in which popular culture became ever more knowing and ever more infantile, taking increasing delight in the indulgent disinterment of earlier pop culture while placing ever higher value on the explicit acknowledgment of the operations of brand and genre. From *The Simpsons* (first aired in 1989) to *Pulp Fiction* (1994), *American Psycho* (published in 1991) to *Scream* (1996), this 'magpieism' took on a new mainstream dominance, although the postmodern notion of using references as substance – the literary and film-making versions of music sampling – stretches back much further. Unsurprising, then, that *The Big Lebowski*'s 1990s setting does not have an altogether cohesive feel. Explicitly riffing off the Chandler stories of the 1930s and 1940s and featuring dream sequences inspired by movie fantasias of the same period, it also evokes the 1950s and 1960s through fetishistic shots of classic 'Brunswick' bowling designs and space-age 'Googie' architecture, while its characters are patently defined by the late 1960s and, to a lesser extent, the 1970s and 1980s. The net experience is less like watching a period piece than being trapped in one of the Dude's occasional acid flashbacks – or rather a nesting set of them, dispersed across the span of his life.

A similar multiplicity applies to the picture's setting. The Coens have always been shrewd observers of location, each of their films exploring and, to an extent, deriving its overall character from a different part of the United States – or at least the *idea* of these American landscapes. The dog-eat-dog Texas of *Blood Simple* contrasts with the Looney Tunes desert of *Raising Arizona* and the leafily handsome anonymous Eastern town in *Miller's Crossing*

(1990, in fact shot in New Orleans); *The Hudsucker Proxy*'s proxy Manhattan is a shimmering notion of hard-headed aspiration, while *Fargo*'s snowy nothings plausibly inspire bleak desperation or Middle-American banality. Later, *O Brother* and *The Ladykillers* (2004) would be founded on different conceptions of Mississippi. *The Big Lebowski* isn't the Coens' only Los Angeles film: *Barton Fink* (1991) had offered a clammy, narcissistic nightmare of Hollywood interiors and *Intolerable Cruelty* (2003) would present a vacuously opulent, sun-kissed Beverly Hills. But *Lebowski* showcases a city where real people live. Joel Coen has referred to the locations of *Lebowski* as characteristic of 'a more marginal Los Angeles – Venice Beach, the Valley, Pasadena – which, in people's minds, isn't really part of the city'.[12]

The result is unusually naturalistic in terms of its geography, offering up neighbourhoods and locations rarely showcased by the industry that practises on their doorstep. Only the scenes in the Dude's bungalow and the dream sequences were shot on constructed sets. The rest of the film lights upon existing sites, though these were often recontextualised in the process: the Star Lanes bowling alley, for instance, was repainted and adorned with star motifs, while the house used as Jackie Treehorn's beach pad is,

Brunswick style: the Star Lanes bowling alley

in fact, located some way inland.[13] By aspiring to an account of the city that does some kind of justice to its sprawling, myriad contents, *The Big Lebowski* offers a more ramshackle, diverse feel. 'The cultures in Los Angeles are more isolated from each other than in New York because of that huge surface spread,' Joel notes. 'All of those sub-cultures are juxtaposed without really communicating.'[14] Richard Schickel wrote of *Double Indemnity*: 'landscape is character. You could charge L.A. as a co-conspirator in the crimes the movie relates.'[15] *Lebowski* invokes the same principle for precisely the opposite effect.

Plaid on plaid

Uncommunicative juxtaposition also forms the frayed, barely continent, yet somehow functional DNA of *The Big Lebowski*. As well as its eclectic approach to look, location and period, the film holds scores of other interesting clashes: the Dude's poster of Nixon bowling, for instance, records a photo op co-ordinated precisely to cast the President in an unexpected light, while his baseball T-shirt has the All-American sport signified by a Japanese star, Sadaharu Oh. Furthermore, according to costume designer Mary Zophres, the item was deliberately placed in the most incongruous scene. 'To me, Jeff

Clashing interestingly: the Dude channels Nixon

looked really stupid in the shirt. He looked, like, "ahhh-duhhh!" in it. So to me, the great-room scene [with the ransom note] was the most appropriate place, because the Dude so doesn't know what's going on.'[16]

The most striking case studies in conspicuous variety are the two dream sequences, comprising elements ostensibly derived from things the Dude has seen or heard and combined without too much concern for rational cohesion – sequences comparable in their effect to the movie's trailer. The first, shorter dream is relatively straightforward, coming after the Dude is knocked unconscious during the invasion of his bungalow by Maude and her art-thugs in search of the rug he lifted from the Lebowski mansion. The knockout prompts a burst of fireworks whose sparks coalesce into the pinprick lights of nocturnal L.A., over which the Dude magically flies; a pastiche of the flying carpet sequence from *The Thief of Bagdad* (1940) then develops into a bowling-themed nightmare expressing feelings of inadequacy, jeopardy and foreboding. The score is Dylan's 'The Man in Me' – the 'Bob' on the B-side of the tape on the Dude's Walkman at the time he is knocked out.

The second dream sequence follows the same transition from ecstatic exuberance to helpless dread but is far more complex, forming a mini-movie in its own right, presented suggestively in the theatre of the Dude's mind as *Gutterballs*. The introductory credits and the Dude's cut-off beige utility suit clearly refer to the *Logjammin'* porn video he has seen, while Saddam Hussein has been conflated with the moustachioed bowling attendant briefly glimpsed during *The Big Lebowski*'s opening credits; the black-and-white

chequered floor is modelled after the tiling in the Lebowski mansion. The appearance of co-ordinated chorines suggests the Dude has seen at least a couple of Busby Berkeley movies. 1930s *Whoopee!*, with its dude-ranch theme, would be a likely candidate: Berkeley's first film as dance director, it pioneered his use of geometrically arranged aerial views and through-the-legs tracking shots.

Maude's Valkyrie get-up, meanwhile, recalls the opera to which the Big Lebowski was listening during the Dude's second visit – 'Wagnerian music' in the script, though Korngold in the final film. But Maude's look seems closer to the pastiche Wagner-world of Chuck Jones's *What's Opera, Doc?* (1957) than any legit production.

The Dude might have been watching *Whoopee!* and *What's Opera, Doc?*

The Big Lebowski is very much in the spirit of that Bugs Bunny cartoon – a lovingly informed parody of a highly codified established form, whose gleeful subversion of genre expectations is matched by genuine emotional resonance. The wish-fulfilment set-up of the Dude coaching Maude in bowling technique offers the only instance in the film where he is in any position of superiority to her, as well an insight into his rather sweet, harmless and somewhat pathetic idea of a freewheeling erotic fantasy. Things take a turn for the worse with a flash of a falling nude girl – the vision that greeted the Dude on his arrival at Jackie Treehorn's – and the appearance of the Johnson-jeopardising nihilists, who have taken up the giant scissors featured in Maude's none-too-subtle castration-themed painting.

The film ensures that its characters also clash in interesting ways, like plaid on plaid. The effect is exacerbated by having many of them personally identified with a particularly strange subculture, from faux-European intellectualism to the L.A. version of stately old money, from armchair militarism to plastic youth. Bunny (Tara Reid) doesn't belong in the Lebowski mansion any more than the Stranger belongs in a bowling alley. There's no more blatant or funny example of such clashing than the lead characters of the Dude (Jeff Bridges) and Walter (John Goodman). Quite how a diffidently amiable radical activist turned vocational stoner established a friendship of considerable depth and affection with a bombastically embittered Vietnam veteran is not broached in the movie, but they probably didn't strike it up in 1968. They are polar opposites both politically and temperamentally: the Dude prefers to let things lie, is

unconcerned with rules, demonstrates empathy for others; Walter is violently proactive, anal, socially crippled.

Of course, odd-couple comedy relies on the balanced juxtaposition of contrary characters who can, in concert, function as a sustainable unit when pitted against an external challenge. But by introducing Walter and, especially, the Dude into a social ecosystem of bewildering variety, the story offers such juxtaposition as a challenge in its own right: trying to keep tabs on the odd

Poles apart: Walter and the Dude

multitude that is *The Big Lebowski*'s Los Angeles is no cakewalk for the sober viewer, let alone the chronically baked Dude. From the bubbling, empty cauldron that is the Big Lebowski (David Huddleston) and his oleaginous major-domo Brandt (Philip Seymour Hoffman) to Lebowski's chillily clipped daughter Maude (Julianne Moore) and her sniggering cohort Knox Harrington (David Thewlis); the reassuringly muddle-headed Stranger (Sam Elliott) to the stretched-nylon cockerel Jesus Quintana (John Turturro); the dead-eyed career nihilist-cum-porn star Uli (Peter Stormare) to the placid, perennially under-informed Donny (Steve Buscemi), it's a constant wonder that such a variety of exotic species inhabit the same planet, let alone the same extended social circuit. When, a full ninety minutes into the action, a new investigator appears (played by Coen regular Jon Polito) and throws another name into the mix, we can only share the Dude's exasperation: 'Who the fuck are the Knutsons?!'

That turns out to be a pretty easy one, though their daughter is harder to pin down: Minnesota teenager Fawn Knutson is better known as Bunny Lebowski, but also goes by the porn name of Bunny La Joya. Hers is not the only blurred, fudged or multiple identity: just about every character in the film turns out to be more or less than they appear. Bunny's husband's 'great man' persona is eventually revealed as hollow grandstanding. 'Father's weakness is vanity,' Maude sniffs, but there's also something unmistakably put on about her own faux-Fluxus artistic preening and strange, supranational speech – what Ethan Coen calls 'a vague, non-specific geographically, swell-finishing-school-for-girls-in-Switzerland accent that [Julianne Moore] came up with'.[17] The Germans – led by Uli Kunkel, aka Karl Hungus – have worked their way from stultifying technopop musicians ('nushing!') and unconvincing nihilists ('it's not fair!') to even less convincing hard men ('ve sreaten you!'). Jackie Treehorn keeps the real nature of his activities at arm's length by insisting, 'I deal in publishing, entertainment, political advocacy.' Other characters turn out to have sexual

A Fawn and two Bunnys, all in one package

identities at odds with their projected selves: Jesus Quintana's hypermacho posturing is undermined by the revelation that he's a 'pederast', while Bunny mischievously hints that the prim Brandt is a voyeur. Even the Stranger seems a little too keen on the Dude: 'I like your style,' he drawls suggestively – and do *real* cowboys drink sarsaparilla...? Walter is almost pathologically sensitive to fakers, singling out Bunny, the Big Lebowski, Quintana and the Germans as fundamentally phoney. Yet his own much-vaunted Judaism is put on (sincerely acquired, but inauthentically Jewish), and he effectively poses as a cop to gain an invitation to the Sellers household. Donny's identity – never strongly expressed – is further weakened by the constantly changing names embroidered onto his thrift-store bowling shirts. Even the Dude goes by an assumed name: as the Stranger informs us, Jeffrey Lebowski 'was the handle his lovin' parents gave him, but he never had much use for it himself'.

Tying the room together
The Big Lebowski's characters are, then, predominantly poseurs of one kind or another, using consciously constructed if not downright misleading personae as a way of going about their business without

'I like your style...' Is even the Stranger all he appears?

having to expose or even acknowledge their 'essential' selves; 'nobody knows anybody', as Tom Regan (Gabriel Byrne) puts it in *Miller's Crossing*. It's paradoxical, then – if further proof of the Coens' own magpie tendency – that the lead characters are, in fact, rooted in reality. 'There are more elements that are actually true in *The Big Lebowski* than there were in *Fargo*,' Joel has said. '*Fargo*, which was allegedly based on real events, in truth contains mostly made-up stuff. Whereas *The Big Lebowski*, which purports to be fiction, actually is based on real people and events.'[18] William Preston Robertson identifies several individuals as particularly inspirational: Joel recalls a seminal encounter with Pete Exline, a somewhat touchy Vietnam vet who was conspicuously proud of 'this ratty-ass little rug he had in his living room... and how it "tied the room together"'.[19] *I'm A Lebowski, You're A Lebowski* – a terrific exploration of the movie's cult appeal, written by the founders of the Lebowski Fest – contains a treasure trove of interviews with people whose stories found their way into the film. In it, Exline, a film producer and professor at the University of Southern California whom the Coens have known since the start of their career, recalls repeatedly mentioning his rug while telling them the story of his car being stolen and recovered and how – with the assistance of his close friend, 'Big'

This is a true story

Lew Abernathy, a bullish Vietnam vet turned private investigator – he traced a piece of homework left in the car back to a junior high school student. Arriving at the student's home, they discovered his sick father – a Hollywood screenwriter – in a hospital bed in their front room. The kid, Jaik Freeman, was unintimidated, even when Abernathy whipped out the homework in a plastic baggie.[20] The character of Walter was also partly inspired by the gung-ho Hollywood figure of John Milius, writer on *Apocalypse Now* (1979) and director of *Conan the Barbarian* (1982) and *Red Dawn* (1984) – and also the California surfing epic *Big Wednesday* (1978). Perhaps the best-known real-world source for the film's characters is Jeff Dowd, former pot-smoking radical and sometime movie producer who goes by the handle 'the Dude' and was indeed a member of the Seattle Seven, as Lebowski claims to have been.

This offbeat concatenation of contrasting yet oddly complementary characteristics formed the germ of the film – and had

Jeff Dowd and John Milius

L.A. written all over it. 'All the characters are pretty much emblematic of Los Angeles,' Ethan notes. 'They're all types who seem like people you would meet there.'[21] (What's more, 'you wouldn't see them in New York'.[22]) As David Thomson has observed of the original *Big Sleep* novel, 'Chandler feels we're on a fault zone here, that many successful Angelenos need to learn a way of overlooking their own past and back story.'[23] Take Bunny: it's not just that she seems to get through selves like other teenagers do clothes or favourite bands, it's as if she's in perpetual flight from any constant identity. Even a Minnesota cheerleader knows that the place to go to reinvent yourself is L.A., a town whose very existence is testament to the will to conjure something from nothing, coax a garden from the desert, and do it your way – even if that means the picking-up and foisting together of mismatched elements, like the rows of incongruous houses in the Hollywood Hills. Further up the coast lies Hearst Castle – the model, of course, for the Xanadu of Charles Foster Kane, who in turn was one of the models for the character of the Big Lebowski – where Spanish cathedral and Doge's palace are fused with Roman baths and ketchup bottles are neatly arranged beneath the refectory arras. It might be utterly derivative, but it's also the expression of a personal sensibility in pursuit of clashing impulses: the grandiosity of material display; the humility of aesthetic deference.

Notions of putting-on also characterise *The Big Lebowski*'s soundtrack. The film's music broadly follows the tack – popularised by Tarantino in *Reservoir Dogs* (1992) and *Pulp Fiction* – of scoring a movie with 'found' pop songs rather than an original composition, a process overseen in this instance by T-Bone Burnett, who would also co-ordinate the phenomenally successful soundtrack for *O Brother, Where Art Thou?* Carter Burwell also composed six or seven short incidental musical sequences for *Lebowski*, including the delicious nihilist technopop pastiche supposedly from Autobahn's album *Nagelbett*, meaning 'bed of nails'. Around thirty tracks were chosen altogether, on several

different bases. 'The premise of the music in the movie', Burwell has said, 'is that this character, Jeff Lebowski, kind of scores his own life with his 8-track collection.'[24] This certainly holds true for the music the Dude is shown listening to diegetically: Captain Beefheart, Bob Dylan, Creedence Clearwater Revival *et al*. Other tracks offer moods associated with specific characters – what Ethan Coen has called 'a musical signature'.[25] The Stranger is associated with Roy Rogers and the Sons of the Pioneers' kitschy 'Tumbling Tumbleweeds', Maude with Meredith Monk's breathy, atonal 'Walking Song', Jackie Treehorn with Mancini's lounge anthem 'Lujon' and Bunny with Esquivel's bouncily flirtatious 'Mucha Muchacha' (too much of a girl indeed, both in terms of her voluptuous persona and her actual schoolgirl status).

These certainly add an additional layer to the characterisations, but the music taps into putting-on more directly. Most obviously, many of the songs are cover versions: we hear Nina Simone and Santana singing songs first written and performed by Duke Ellington and Tito Puente respectively, as well as Townes Van Zandt's version of the Stones' 'Dead Flowers' and two covers of 'Viva Las Vegas'. The Dude loses his seat in a cab by objecting on principle – even when injured – to the Eagles' ironically enervating 'Peaceful Easy

Feeling', but the cliché that is 'Hotel California' is redeemed by the hypnotic, almost diabolic use to which the Gipsy Kings' version of the track is put as backdrop to Quintana's celebratory dance routine. There are further musical hints at co-opted subjects and constructed identities: the Dude's landlord Marty's (Jack Kehler) performance cycle, for instance, is set to 'Gnomus' from Mussorgsky's *Pictures at an Exhibition*, making it a dance based on an orchestral arrangement of a piano piece based on a design for a nutcracker shaped like a gnome. The Big Lebowski uses classical music to imply a narrative around Bunny's disappearance, first listening – somewhat peremptorily – to Mozart's *Requiem*, and then – even more peremptorily – to Korngold's opera *City of the Dead*, in which a widower comes to terms with the death of his young wife. 'Just Dropped In (To See What Condition My Condition Was In)' proves the perfect accompaniment to the Dude's major dream sequence. A psychedelic rock track written, tongue somewhat in cheek, by Mickey Newbury, it was a hit in 1968 for Kenny Rogers and the New Edition, who soon afterwards established the country folk identity with which they were much more closely associated, and more comfortable.[26] Even Creedence were a bunch of Californians pretending to be from the Deep South.

In the parlance of our times

A more literal magpieism – the picking up and passing on of tropes or gobbets with little concern for context or meaning – is also a leitmotif of *The Big Lebowski*'s dialogue. Its most obvious expression is the questionable citation of supposedly learned sources in which some characters indulge. The Stranger, for instance, offers a couple of dollops of dubious folk wisdom attributed to unidentified 'fellers' ('I ain't never seen no queen in her damned undies, as the feller said'; 'a wiser feller than m'self once said, "Sometimes you eat the bar and... sometimes the bar, well, he eats you"'), while Walter quotes Shakespeare, Herzl and Talmudic lore in circumstances with scant relevance to the original context. The

Dude also has a go, though attribution proves to be a tricky game when Donny's around:

DUDE   It's all goddamn fake, man. It's like Lenin said, you look for the person who will benefit and, uh, uh, you know –
DONNY   I am the Walrus.
DUDE   You know, you'll, uh – You know what I'm trying to say.
DONNY   I am the Walrus.
WALTER   That fucking bitch!
DUDE   Yeah.
DONNY   I am the Walrus.
WALTER   Shut the fuck up, Donny! V. I. Lenin! Vladimir Ilyich Ulyanov!
DONNY   What the fuck is he talking about?

Lenin said something vaguely along these lines, but the Dude in fact seems to be thinking of *cui bono*, the maxim Cicero attributed to Cassius. Donny, meanwhile, thinks of his 'Lennon' in terms of a Beatles song, while, in the overlapping, perfectly timed comic gibberish of the film, Walter rants about the spoiled rich; each is lost in his own world. Such is the fug of questionability that pervades the film, from the initial misidentification of the Dude as the other Jeffrey Lebowski to the Dude's own mistaking the nihilists' ferret for a marmot or the reference to Cynthia's dog – a terrier – as a Pomeranian.

Just as inaccurate quotation can be a substitute for considered argument, some words and phrases take on through repetition a talismanic quality that seems a substitute for thoughtfulness.

Intolerable Cruelty (left) features a Pomeranian. *The Big Lebowski* (right) does not

The notion that the Dude's rug 'really tied the room together', for instance, is as close as he gets to a righteous justification for his crusade. Having mentioned this attribute after the initial incident, the phrase is repeated by Donny, as a question, and by Walter, as *casus belli*. The Dude then uses it in his initial approach to the Big Lebowski, and returns to it as a kind of lodestar at such key moments as his drugging by Jackie Treehorn.[27] Plenty of other dialogue is passed from character to character with scant regard for considered applicability. Take the language used by George H. W. Bush in a news report about the Iraqi invasion of Kuwait overheard by the Dude at the end of the opening scene. 'This aggression will not stand,' the President insists as the Dude helps himself to some half-and-half. A few scenes later, during his first encounter with the Big Lebowski, the Dude reapplies this sabre-rattling of a world leader to rug-pissing (an activity already described by Walter as 'unchecked aggression'), maintaining that 'this will not stand, ya know? This will not stand, man!' The Dude also magpies the nihilists' pet phrase 'no funny stuff' when trying to reassure Jackie Treehorn of his bona fides, and parrots Maude's qualification 'in the parlance of our times' to the Big Lebowski in an inept attempt to avoid offence.

The Lebowski household evinces a tendency to use such repetition deliberately to drum a given idea into the Dude's apparently childlike head. Maude assures him twice within a few seconds that her recommended doctor is 'a good man, and thorough'. During his ostensible dark night of the soul, the Big Lebowski, trying to imbue his words with resonance, pointedly repeats his portentous dictum that 'strong men also cry'. Once the Dude commits to his new task, its seriousness is repeatedly reiterated.

BRANDT   Her life is in your hands.

DUDE   Oh, man, don't say that.

BRANDT   Mr Lebowski asked me to repeat that: her life is in your hands.

DUDE   Shit.

BRANDT   Her life is in your hands, Dude.

The tactic seems to rub off: following the botched handover, the Dude reminds Walter that 'her life was in our hands!' The Big Lebowski duly bellows it once more in the back of his limo. The Dude shortly develops his own new catchphrase – 'they're going to kill that poor woman!' – with which Walter becomes so familiar that he ends up ridiculing it through sing-song mimicry. Nor is this the only time that repetition of a phrase diminishes its impact: can we still take seriously Brandt's assessment of Nancy Reagan as a 'wonderful woman' once he has described jailbait porn queen Bunny the same way? 'Is this your homework, Larry?' becomes inanely ineffectual through its five repetitions, just as, by the fifth time the nihilists warn against the consequences of 'funny stuff', it's clear there's little to worry about. Other phrases seem simply to be floating in the ether, used by characters with no obvious connection to one another: both Treehorn's thug and Walter, for instance, are fond of the confrontational phrase 'you see what happens?'; both the Dude and the Big Lebowski use the term 'Chinaman'; both Maude and Uli use 'Johnson' as a euphemism for penis; both the Chief of Police of Malibu and Walter take exception to another character's 'goldbricking ass'. The overall effect is to suggest a kind of endemic recycling, as if the state's water or power shortages might also apply to thoughts and words.

If in real need, swear. This is, of course, one of the most efficient linguistic methods of achieving maximum impact with minimum imagination, and *The Big Lebowski* is a remarkably profane film. 'Sure, "fuck it!"' as the Big Lebowski says. 'That's your answer to everything!' According to the Family Media Guide (a conservative watchdog website that itemises elements of films some parents might find objectionable), the movie uses the word 'fuck' and its derivatives more than 260 times – on average, once every twenty-five seconds – along with other profanities including, but not limited to, thirty-seven shits, six assholes, two bitches and a bastard.[28] All in all, it's quite possibly the sweariest comedy set in Los Angeles County, which would place it high in the running for sweariest worldwide. Little wonder that the notably strait-laced Stranger asks the Dude 'd'ya *have* to use so many cuss words?'

There are moments that render swearing impressively cogent by comparison, when ambition outstrips articulation and the attempt to ape a higher register ends in bluster or nonsense. The tone is set by the Stranger's opening narration: 'Sometimes there's a man... Sometimes there's a man... Wal, I lost m'train of thought here, but – Aw hell, I done innerduced him enough.' Soon after, this trend continues with Walter's astounding bowling-alley attempt to clarify his point: 'Huh? No! What the fuck are *you* talking – I'm not – We're not – We're talking about unchecked aggression here!' Later he notes 'that keeping wildlife, um, an amphibious rodent for, um, you know, domestic – within the city – That ain't legal either.' Brandt too has moments of uncertainty: 'That's a Los Angeles Chamber of Commerce Business Achiever award, which is given – not necessarily given every year, given only when there's a worthy – somebody especially –' But few can hold a candle to the Dude for sheer inarticulacy. Take the scene in the back of the Big Lebowski's limo, following the botched handover:

DUDE   Those guys are – We dropped off the damn money.

BIG LEBOWSKI *We?!*

DUDE   I. The royal we, you know, the editorial – I dropped off the money exactly as per – Look, man, I've got certain information, all right, certain things have come to light and – You know, has it ever occurred to you that instead of, uh, you know, running around, uh, uh, blaming me, you know, given the nature of all this new shit, you know, it, it, it, this could be a, a, a lot more, uh, uh, uh, uh, uh, uh, complex – I mean it's not just, it might not be just such a simple, uh – You know?

BIG LEBOWSKI What in God's holy name are you blathering about?

Conversely, Maude, though highly articulate, repeatedly finds herself aping a strange version of the vernacular – 'the parlance of our times' – referring to dollars as 'bones or clams or whatever you call them', as if holding the offending vocabulary at arm's length between pinched fingernails. But at least she's trying to engage – in this world of stunted, half-cocked communication, the important thing is to make the effort. Nothing is more frustrating than opting out altogether – hence the apoplectic rage of both Walter and the usually mild-mannered Dude in the face of Larry Sellers' impassivity. Throughout his extended interrogation, the kid doesn't say peep.

There isn't a literal connection

An actual constructive engagement with the use of language – an interrogation of meaning – is far harder to find. To his credit, and despite his copious willingness to blather and bullshit on occasion, the Dude also has a tendency to throw unfamiliar words back in people's faces when taken by surprise ('coitus?', 'Johnson?', 'employed?') – a willingness to admit ignorance, and therefore question meaning, endearingly shared by Donny ('What's a pederast, Walter?'). The Dude will express wry scepticism ('He's a nihilist.' 'That must be exhausting') and even directly challenge ambiguity and dissembling. When Jackie Treehorn sniffily claims to be involved only in publishing and advocacy work, the Dude asks, 'Which one was *Logjammin'*?' and when Walter tries to bring his military experience into the conversation, yet again, the Dude picks him up on it.

DUDE   I don't see any connection to Vietnam, Walter.

WALTER   Well, there isn't a literal connection, Dude.

DUDE   Walter, face it, there isn't *any* connection. It's your roll.

This tendency – occasional and mild as it might be – to take issue with lies and *non sequiturs* establishes the Dude as a rare bird in his surroundings, a character who takes meaning seriously. It's also noteworthy in this context that the Dude is responsible for perhaps the only instance in the movie of a phrase gaining rather than losing resonance through repetition. 'Where's the money, Lebowski?' opens the film's very first exchange of dialogue, and it signifies ignorance on the part of Treehorn's goon. When the Dude uses the same line storming into the Lebowski mansion at the climax of the mystery, we have come full circle, only this time the house invasion is founded on logic and solid understanding.

The Big Lebowski might be a thing of rags and patches, then, but it's not simply an extended exercise in hollow pastiche; rather it's a film *about* pastiche, about sampling, magpieism, the putting on of identities, the patchwork nature of Los Angeles – and about the movies themselves. For among its plurality of incongruities, not the least is its cavalier approach to genre. We open, don't forget, with Roy Rogers and his boys crooning over clippity-cloppity music, credits appearing in painted-wagon lettering over a desert tracking shot, and Sam Elliott's cowboy voice telling us that 'way out West, there was this feller, feller I wanna tell you about'. Plainly, this is a Western. 'Feller by the name of Jeff Lebowski,' he continues – not, admittedly, a stereotypical gunslinger's name, but then he does admit 'there was a lot about the Dude that didn't make a whole lot of sense to me', and there's a ball of tumbleweed to keep us anchored in the genre. Then a drum rumbles ominously beneath the song and we mount the crest of a hill to reveal the nocturnal glitter of Los Angeles sprawl. Hmm. Not a Western, then. Yet we're still following that tumbleweed, along a bridge over a freeway, down a street, past a burrito stand and onto the beach itself. Tumbleweed on the beach? What kind of movie is this anyway?

The set-up that unrolls in the opening few scenes – the invasion of the Dude's home, the audience with the other Jeffrey Lebowski – establishes that, in fact, we're in noir territory; a chucklesome improbability given the Dude's evident unsuitability to the task of entrepreneurial investigator, which makes about as much sense as … well, as tumbleweed on the beach, or the credits' marriage of that

Western typeface with chrome Cadillac-style lettering. Yet as the plot unfolds it becomes clear that the incongruities go deeper than this central miscasting: Walter's crucial influence over the plot and the centrality of his and the Dude's co-dependent friendship means that, in Joel's words, 'this story is in fact that of a marriage, an odd couple'.[29] As Ethan puts it, 'it is, in a strange way, kind of a buddy movie'.[30] While you wouldn't expect to find noir and the Western sandwiched into the same film, the genres at least have a shared vision of masculinity, developing the American notion of the hero as 'a man alone'. But buddy movie and film noir? Are there two genres with less compatible views of human nature – the one predicated on the durability of social bonds, the other on their fallibility? Now *that*'s an odd couple. *The Big Lebowski* is not just the story of a ransom gone wrong, it's also a case study in genre gone wrong, genre gone wild, gone fishing or gone bowling.

A Western. Right ...?

2 Out of the Past

Six Coen brothers films to date take the crime genre as their point of departure – *Blood Simple*, *Miller's Crossing*, *Fargo*, *The Big Lebowski*, *The Man Who Wasn't There* and *The Ladykillers* – and several others, like *Raising Arizona*, contain subplots involving criminal intrigues.[31] The registers of *Blood Simple* and *Miller's Crossing* might be described as homage to or updating of classic crime; these films are relatively 'straight' in mood, and recall the pulp classics of James M. Cain and Dashiell Hammett respectively. The very different tones of *The Man Who Wasn't There* and *Fargo*, by contrast, involve a rich and strange mixture of slyness and seriousness, falling more clearly into the category of 'ironic noir', films with an arch, self-conscious or subversive intent. *The Man Who Wasn't There*, for example, at first glance seems to adhere to the fatalism and brooding, shadowy moral world of classic noir. But in fact its main character, Ed Crane (Billy Bob Thornton), rather than being trapped by fate or a femme fatale, actually allows others around him to suffer without lifting a finger to help anyone when it matters. This makes the film almost an inversion of the plot of *Double Indemnity*, just as *The Big Lebowski* is in several important ways a sustained subversion of *The Big Sleep* (whose screenplay was co-written by William Faulkner and Leigh Brackett). The transition from the Coens' earlier crime films to these later titles is notable for a remarkable range of moods and styles, as well as an increasing emphasis on comedy. In Ethan Coen's 1998 book of short stories, *Gates of Eden*, several of the tales are send-ups of the hard-boiled genre; in 'Hector Berlioz, Private Detective,' the PI tells his client 'I have a temp in when there's heavy gunplay.'[32]

The Ladykillers, a translation of the 1955 Ealing crime comedy to the contemporary American South, is the only actual Coen remake to date. But in a sense, most of the Coens' films have been 'retro-remakes' of one sort or another, often of classic but discarded Hollywood material from the 1940s, like the fast-talking newsroom comedy (*The Hudsucker Proxy*), the screwball (*Raising Arizona*) or, on a far more specific level, Preston Sturges' idiosyncratic 1941 masterpiece *Sullivan's Travels* (*O Brother, Where Art Thou?*). Unsurprising, then, despite their greater range of source material, to find the Coens linked with Quentin Tarantino, David Mamet and other 1990s noir recyclers.[33]

It is worth noting that much of the fun of mainstream 1990s cinema is missed by taking a purely pejorative understanding of the term 'pastiche'. Imitating the style of previous works and the deployment of a hyper-allusive technique is not only quintessentially postmodern but also formed aspects of a running commentary on the Hollywood system itself for many of these film-makers. Critic Stephen Hunter describes 'the ironic stage of noir' as a shared style with 'the cool, detached humor of a good movie review, which in a

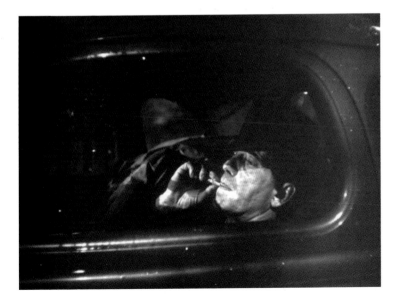

Bogarting: *The Big Sleep*

sense it is'.[34] Hunter argues that 'nouveau' or 'neo'-noir's rise to prominence occurred in the years following the success of Lawrence Kasdan's *Body Heat* (1981). But the pedigree of ironic noir as a mini-tradition playing with the conventions of the genre stretches back through Robert Altman's *The Long Goodbye* (1973) and John Huston's *Beat the Devil* (1953, co-scripted by Truman Capote) to the most striking early precursor, the *Thin Man* series (1934–47) that riffs on Hammett. Raymond Borde and Étienne Chaumeton identified a series of films that indulged in parodies of the genre, including Richard Wallace's *It's In the Bag* (1945), Elliott Nugent's *My Favorite Brunette* (1947, featuring Bob Hope), Lloyd Bacon's *The Fuller Brush Girl* (1950), Sidney Lanfield's *The Lemon Drop Kid* (1951) and George Beck's *Behave Yourself* (1951).[35] We could also add John Farrow's *His Kind of Woman* (1951). At the time of noir's revival, Carl Reiner's *Dead Men Don't Wear Plaid* (1982) had Steve Martin quipping back to vintage footage, while Jake Kasdan's *Zero Effect* (1998), released in the same year as *Lebowski*, used Bill Pullman effectively as a basket-case sleuth.

Not everyone has been thrilled with the Coen aesthetic of replaying, mixing and scratching all the classic records in the collection. Pauline Kael dismissed *Blood Simple* as 'a Hollywood by-product', and, what was more annoying to Kael, a by-product produced by directors independent of the system.[36] But 'Hollywood by-product' is not a bad description of many good commercial films made in America in the 1990s, including Mamet's *Homicide* (1991), Tarantino's *Pulp Fiction*, Spike Lee's *Clockers* (1995), Wes Anderson's *Bottle Rocket* (1996), David Fincher's *The Game* (1997) and Curtis Hanson's *L.A. Confidential* (1997). These were essentially new variations on the mystery/crime/detective/conman/thriller picture; some were relatively straight, but most were ironic or subversive of the genre on some level. Even though these films don't always mimic the expressionist style or fatalistic worldview specifically associated with classic noir, they represented a resurgence of the crime genre during the high-water mark of postmodernist kitsch.

Barbet Schroeder, who readapted *Kiss of Death* in 1995 (it had previously been shot by Henry Hathaway in 1957), once described the retro technique of 1990s neo-noir as being similar to 'a painter who tries to rework and explore the classics'.[37] In *Blood Simple*, a similar process works by updating the mood of a Cain dime novel of adultery and murder, whereas *Miller's Crossing* manages to create the breathtaking impression that it is a film adaptation of a lost Dashiell Hammett novel. Yet if previous Coen efforts might be likened to new and somewhat mannered paintings in the style of the Old Masters, *The Big Lebowski* is more like Marcel Duchamp's addition of a moustache and obscene graffiti to Da Vinci's *Mona Lisa* in the readymade *L.H.O.O.Q.* The film is, among other things, a defacing of the work of the greatest of the 'old masters' of the American detective story, Raymond Chandler.

Chandler, greatly influenced by Hammett and the *Black Mask* magazine writing of the era Hammett helped pioneer, brought a trademark wit and fleet literary style to the 'tough-guy school' of American fiction, in the process creating one of the great characters of the detective genre, Philip Marlowe. Marlowe, a scrupulous and solitary man immersed in a depraved and corrupt Los Angeles world, loved razor wit, chess and hard liquor. He was Chandler's knight errant, set to wade into the muck of trouble without having his integrity befouled. Chandler's pure stylishness and Marlowe's grim but determined worldview – a Romantic heart clouded in veils of pessimism thick as pipe smoke – helps explain the endurance of both of them in the Hollywood imagination as the twentieth-century American Sherlock Holmes.

The obviously affectionate playfulness with which the Coens lay waste to Chandler's oeuvre and worldview in *Lebowski* is perhaps best seen as a strange type of homage. It was logical for the Coens to move from Cain and Hammett to Chandler, almost systematically exploring the nooks and crannies of the classic pulp-detective genre, sometimes reproducing and sometimes satirising its salient features. The choice of target is made more appropriate because of Chandler's towering influence on the development of noir as a Hollywood film genre. The godfather of 'the high budget mystery picture trend', as Chandler himself once put it, wrote or co-wrote the scripts for *Double Indemnity*, *The Blue Dahlia* (1946) and *Strangers on a Train* (1951).[38] His own fiction, meanwhile, provided the source material for the classic film adaptations of *Farewell, My Lovely* (filmed in 1944 as *Murder, My Sweet*), *Lady in the Lake* (1947) and *The Big Sleep*, as well as a multitude of later productions. Chandler shared the Coens' scepticism about Hollywood as a place where literature could flourish (as in *Barton Fink*), but he and Billy Wilder created out of Cain's *Double Indemnity* a new and formative kind of cinema.

To tease Chandler posthumously, then, is essentially to tease the Hollywood detective film and, in some sense, to tease Hollywood and perhaps film history itself. In *Fargo*, the detective formula is served up soft-boiled, whereas in *The Big Lebowski* the effect is more like throwing an egg at a beloved icon. If it is possible to egg someone lovingly, that is essentially what the Coens are doing to Chandler. *The Big Lebowski* is a most playful parricide, one in which the satire always plays along with the comedy, so that the multitudinous references and tangent lines from other films never seem intrusive or overly nerdy. The ultimate point is not to comment on film history but to make people laugh.

Dick amuck

The central conceit of *Fargo*, like *Lebowski*, is the notion of an incongruous sleuth playing havoc with the classic conventions of the detective story. (*Lebowski* was actually written first, but its production was delayed by John Goodman's television commitments on *Roseanne*.[39]) The very pregnant small-town detective Marge Gunderson (Frances McDormand), who vomits when she discovers corpses not from queasiness but morning sickness, conforms neither to the tough-guy paradigm nor to the stereotype of the *ingénue* caught up in a terrifying intrigue beyond her control and then

rescued by a real man. Instead, she's a sensible, smart woman,
thoroughly up to the task confronting her, who solves her case not
by unravelling esoteric riddles or roughing up a series of recalcitrant
informants but following procedure. Marge is a nice, normal
Minnesotan hometown girl doing her job in a professional but
decidedly unrushed manner.

The notion of an incongruous or even amateur sleuth forced to
solve a mystery was already a classic trope of the suspense genre,
Hitchcock's *North by Northwest* (1959) providing the quintessential

The Dude and Marge Gunderson: offbeat, rotund sleuths

plot in which the wrong man is involved in intrigue through a case of mistaken identity and must rise to the task. *Lebowski* lifts something of this conceit to start the engine of its plot, as well as mocking the technique used in Hitchcock's film to expose impressions of previous writing on pads of paper. You also get a sense of the Coens' mischief by contrasting the efficient quick thinking through which Cary Grant's Roger Thornhill neutralises the threat of the crop duster with the panicked yelp with which the Dude greets the aerial bombardment of Maude's painting technique.

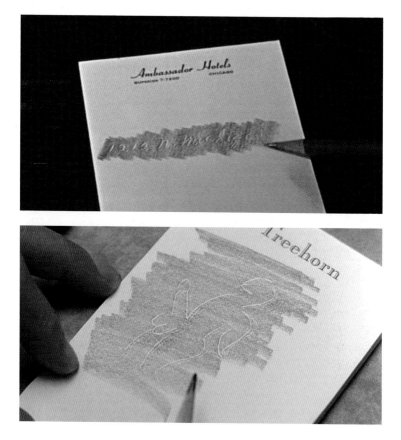

Paper trails in *North by Northwest* (top) and *The Big Lebowski*

There are weird shreds of other films embedded in *Lebowski*, like Ivan Passer's nouveau noir *Cutter's Way* (1981), in which a young, svelte, muscular Jeff Bridges plays a beach bum gigolo with an angry and abusive Vietnam vet pal. The film includes a car-bashing in nocturnal suburbia and a scene in a diner patronised by an Old West old-timer; at its climax, the pair storm the black-and-white-marble-floored mansion of the corrupt bigwig whom they've been investigating. *Cutter's Way*, released in the same year as *Body Heat*,

Bridges in *Cutter's Way* (top) and *The Big Lebowski*

undermined the conventions of the genre far more than Kasdan's noir homage. Asked whether he saw connections beyond the casting of Bridges, scriptwriter Jeffrey Alan Fiskin told the authors: 'Our intention – and that of the Coens as well, I suspect – was to subvert the genre.'

The influence of *The Long Goodbye*, often mentioned by the Coens as their favourite Altman film and an acknowledged precursor of *Lebowski*, is even more sustained. Robertson's description of the relationship between Altman and the Coens is apt:

To Chandler's tough, romantic vision of L.A., Altman and [scriptwriter Leigh] Brackett added a development new to the L.A. landscape since Chandler's passing, but one that was thoroughly consistent with his world: the flake. In *The Long Goodbye*, hard-boiled wit is replaced by hard-boiled nitwit. Terse patter becomes rambling inanities. And the melancholic Marlowe becomes the easygoing Elliot Gould. *The Big Lebowski* picks up where Altman's *The Long Goodbye* left off...[40]

As well as being structured as investigations into crimes that turn out not to have happened at all, both films have early scenes in supermarkets: Marlowe's seemingly trivial and eccentric quest for cat food in *The Long Goodbye* resonates with the Dude's shopping trip to Ralph's for half-and-half in the film's opening scene. *The Long Goodbye* also features a Jewish gangster disgruntled about working on the Sabbath (a central feature of Walter's character in *Lebowski*) and plays on the proximity of the city to the beach. Altman's Marlowe shares the Dude's interest in bowling too.

While Marge Gunderson is an offbeat but serious investigator, the Dude is an anti-noir joke, a fully baked Venice Beach basket-case who does not even know the day of the week, let alone sleuthing procedure. One wonders what Chandler would have made of *The Big Lebowski*, which is supersaturated in quotations from and references to his work and style but relentlessly, exuberantly and hilariously subversive of pretty much everything he believed in. Measured against Chandler's standards of professionalism, the role

the Coens created for Jeff Bridges is a spectacular disgrace, and deliberately so.

In 'The Simple Art of Murder', Chandler famously laid down the law about what kind of guy a detective was supposed to be:

Down these mean streets a man must go who is not himself mean, who is neither tarnished nor afraid. The detective in this kind of story must be such a man. He is the hero, he is everything. He must be a complete man and a common man and yet an unusual man. He must be, to use a rather weathered phrase, a man of honor, by instinct, by inevitability, without thought of it, and certainly without saying it. He must be the best man in his world and a good enough man for any world.[41]

Shopping in L.A.: Gould in *The Long Goodbye* (top) and Bridges in *The Big Lebowski*

A segue into the Stranger's opening monologue about the Dude in *Lebowski* offers a sense of how wickedly Chandlerism is being evoked and mocked simultaneously, even though it comes through the dialect of a cowboy:

Sometimes there's a man – I won't say a hee-ro, 'cause what's a hee-ro? – but sometimes there's a man... Wal, he's the man for his time 'n' place, he fits right in there – and that's the Dude, in Los Angeles... and even if he's a lazy man, and the Dude was certainly that – quite possibly the laziest in Los Angeles County... which would place him high in the runnin' for laziest worldwide – but sometimes there's a man... Sometimes there's a man...

Thus far, with great difficulty and effort, the Stranger has been able to establish only that: a) the Dude is not any kind of recognisable hero; b) the Dude is a basically a wreck of a human being; c) the Dude is, at least biologically speaking, a man; and, finally, d) 'sometimes there's a man'. 'Sometimes there's a man' is surely one of the most accurate, meaningless and funny statements ever made. *Sometimes* there *is* a man, somewhere in the world, doing something or other. So what? This man happens to be shopping in Ralph's supermarket in his tattered bathrobe and writing out whale-illustrated cheques for sixty-nine cents in order to buy half-and-half so that he can mix more White Russians in his Venice bungalow. Jeff Bridges is not exactly Humphrey Bogart's Philip Marlowe; he's a far cry from even Elliot Gould's. He is, however, a Coen type recognisable from *Raising Arizona* and *The Hudsucker Proxy*, a discombobulated, obtuse but somehow lovable loser who is thrust way over his head into a quickly unravelling situation.

In discussions of the genesis of the film, the Coens make clear that one of their intentions was to 'do' Chandler, the way that they had done Hammett and would later more explicitly do Cain. They told Andy Lowe that *Lebowski* is 'a Raymond Chandler thing – a sort of wandering intrigue which explores different parts of the city, through the characters'.[42] In another interview, Michel Ciment and

Hubert Niogret probably got the straightest explanation. Ethan: 'For us it was above and beyond all else a California story. We even drew loose inspiration from a Chandler plot outline. All his novels, or almost all, are situated in Los Angeles.' Joel: 'The logic here is more episodic – like in a Chandler novel, the hero sets out to clear up a mystery and while doing so visits a lot of odd characters who spring up like Jack-in-the-boxes.'[43] Even the homework-in-a-bag scene, based on one of Pete Exline's madcap stories, somehow touched a Chandler chord: 'I remember when Pete told us the story... and then later, in talking to Ethan about it, thinking that there was something quintessentially L.A. about it, but L.A. in a very Chandlerian way.'[44] The Coens have a literary sense of topography: for them, there is something fundamentally Chandlerian about L.A.

Chandler vs Hawks vs Coen

But are we talking about Raymond Chandler the novelist, Raymond Chandler the scriptwriter, or Raymond Chandler as adapted, in notoriously problematic fashion, by Howard Hawks in the Bogart/Bacall version of *The Big Sleep*, in which many of the key elements of Chandler's plot are half-erased, overridden or discarded? On several occasions, the Coens have made clear that they wanted to emphasise the writer, telling Lowe, for example, that 'it was Chandler's novels that inspired *The Big Lebowski*'.[45] That said, Ethan makes a revealing slip in his interview with Ciment and Niogret, a mistake which suggests some blurring between the world of the Chandler novel and the Hawks film. He says that there is in *Lebowski*,

as so often with [Chandler's] novels, a mature and sophisticated woman, Maude, played by Julianne Moore, and a licentious and depraved girl, Bunny, played by Tara Reid. The main character is often involved in a romantic sub-plot with the first type of woman.[46]

In the novel *The Big Sleep*, however, there is no romantic subplot. The closest Marlowe gets to home plate with anybody is actually with the licentious and depraved younger sister, Carmen Sternwood, who turns up naked in his bed and attempts to seduce him. It is only in the film adaptation of *The Big Sleep* that the older sister, Vivian Regan, becomes a commanding presence as the role expands to fill Hawks's obsession with Bacall, and the film becomes more and more about the love affair between Marlowe and Vivian – or even Bogart and Bacall – and less and less about any comprehensible mystery plot.[47] In the classic Marlowe films, including *Murder, My Sweet* and *Lady in the Lake*, the detective always gets the girl; in Chandler, he never does.

This minor mix-up notwithstanding, it is clear from a variety of references that the Coens used Chandler's novels – and not just *The Big Sleep* – to good effect in *Lebowski*. The scene with Carmen Sternwood slipping naked into the detective's apartment actually turns up in a parodic form in *Lebowski*, when Maude breaks into the Dude's bungalow and awaits his return. Presumably she is lying naked in his bed until he stumbles over the piece of wood he nailed into his floor

The Big Sleep's Carmen Sternwood (Martha Vickers)

earlier in a forlorn attempt to prevent break-ins. Then Maude appears hovering above him in his own bathrobe, which she then sheds before seducing him. 'That's my robe,' the Dude remarks, failing to grasp the chain of events that has just occurred, in which Maude has been startled by noises in the next room and hastily thrown on the Dude's robe to investigate. It's a tiny but subtle bit of fun. The numerous home invasions the Dude endures resemble similar episodes in *The Big Sleep*, in which it becomes a running joke that anyone can pick Marlowe's lock and wait in his apartment while he is out.

Several other Chandlerisms specifically from the novels make their way into the film, or almost do, including the tough-guy slang used by the private investigator character Da Fino (Jon Polito) – a role that recalls Elisha Cook's Jones in *The Big Sleep* – about being a 'brother shamus'. When Marlowe is knocked out then drugged in *Farewell, My Lovely*, the narration describes him entering a pool of darkness as follows: 'It had no bottom.' The Stranger uses almost exactly the same words ('there was no bottom') for almost exactly the same situation, after the Dude is drugged by Jackie Treehorn, whose Malibu house somewhat resembles Chandler's description – 'an angular building' – of the secluded mansion belonging to a quack psychic in which Marlowe is beaten and doped.[48] It could also be argued that the pompous language and phoney, imperious style of both the Big Lebowski and Maude resembles that of Mrs Murdock in *The High Window*, who preaches about learning to live on a 'sufficient but not gaudy allowance'.[49] Bunny Lebowski's 'ample' allowance, by comparison, is clearly not ample enough for her voracious needs and necessitates a double life in pornography, also the sideline of Carmen Sternwood in *The Big Sleep*. It's notable, however, that where Carmen's involvement in the industry is a dirty secret that prompts blackmail and murder, Bunny's is an openly acknowledged non-issue.

Hawks's film adaptation of *The Big Sleep* doesn't tower over *Lebowski*; rather, it is subtly embedded and structurally parodied without becoming an overwhelming or distracting presence. That said, the relationship between the two films, and between various dimensions of each film's wider story, is sustained and intriguing. William Faulkner, who co-wrote the script of *The Big Sleep*, had been an earlier target of the Coens in *Barton Fink*, in which W. P. Mayhew (John Mahoney), a Southern writer turned Hollywood hack, is portrayed as a fraudulent drunk whose great novels had actually been written by his female secretary. Hawks's *His Girl Friday*, meanwhile, had provided in Rosalind Russell one of the models for the fast-talking tomboy newspaper writer played by Jennifer Jason Leigh in *The Hudsucker Proxy* (Katharine Hepburn was another).

The Coens' interest in Hawks is interesting insofar as they seem to be such diametrical opposites as film-makers. Hawks was reportedly a manipulative, sexually aggressive, anti-Semitic compulsive liar who, like Faulkner, relied on masculine bluster, phoney self-presentation and a series of acquired identities. Compare this with the Coens, who appear to be happily married family men with undramatic personal lives and an intense dislike of autobiographical questions. Equally, their working modes couldn't be more different. Hawks notoriously loved 'kicking around' a scene until he got it right. The Coens, by contrast, are famously frugal film-makers known for exhaustive storyboarding, a strict and exacting approach to their budget and the cultivation of a relaxed, low-stress on-set environment. Their scripts are basically sacrosanct, and they sometimes retake scenes when an actor deviates from the text even by one word, a fact brought up independently by two longtime Coen collaborators, Jon Polito and Peter Stormare.[50] (Stormare recalled a scene from *Fargo* that required reshooting to ensure the script was followed literally to the letter, his line being 'Where is pancakes house?' and *not* 'Where is pancake house?') Compare this with the almost antic way in which Hawks heedlessly shredded Chandler's text until it quite literally ceased to make sense. Following test screenings, Hawks actually removed from the initial cut of the film a longish scene in which Marlowe explains everything that has happened and, quite brilliantly and understandably, added more Bacall, Bacall, Bacall.

Honolulu cocktails

While the tones of *The Big Sleep* and *The Big Lebowski* are poles apart, in terms of their odd threads between different L.A. social worlds and class strata, their approach to opulent mansions, minxes, butlers, wheelchair-bound grandees, debts owed to pornographers and corrupt women – even their emphasis on the sleuth's car as a reflection of his persona and the relaying of key information by telephone – the two films are running on parallel tracks much of the time, so that comparisons can range from obvious references to minutiae. Walter's pulling out a piece on the lanes, for instance, prompts a gross parody of the kind of hair-trigger stand-off Marlowe

Auto identities: smooth Marlowe, battered Dude

expertly defuses. (The Dude, of course, merely mumbles one or two exasperated, ineffectual complaints.) Among the Coens' more blatant spoofs of Hawks is the great-room scene, in which the Dude learns of the supposed kidnapping of Bunny from a seemingly distraught Big Lebowski. Rick Heinrichs, the production designer, describes the making of the scenic details as a cross between General Sternwood's sweltering greenhouse and 'a bit of a *Citizen Kane* feeling... this pitiful guy in a wheelchair with all this magnificent artwork staring down at him'.[51] While *The Big Sleep* portrays General Sternwood as a decrepit father figure looking for an honourable and manly surrogate son in Marlowe, *Lebowski* undercuts many dimensions of the scene with incongruous analogues. For one thing, unlike the protective Sternwood, the Big Lebowski doesn't care about Bunny's return and actually hopes that the kidnappers will do away with her, a fact he inadvertently reveals through his choice of Mozart's *Requiem* as a diegetic soundtrack for the scene (an apposite late substitution for Wagner's *Lohengrin*, specified in the script).

In *The Big Sleep*, General Sternwood, too sickly to smoke cigars himself, enjoys tobacco vicariously through Marlowe; in *Lebowski*'s great-room scene, the Dude lights up a reefer. (Indeed, *The Big Sleep*'s ubiquitous cigarettes are replaced throughout by the Dude's joints.) Over and against Marlowe's commanding presence, debonair clothing and spot-on appropriateness in dealing with the General, the Dude can only remark, while holding marijuana smoke in the small passages of his lungs, that the apparent kidnapping of Bunny is 'a bummer'. 'Are you surprised at my tears, sir?' asks the Big Lebowski in a moment seeming to call for the most delicate display of empathy; the Dude's impressed response is 'fuckin' A'. In *The Big Sleep*, honourable men have to band together to try to keep wild young girls out of fatal trouble; in *The Big Lebowski*, the phoney exploits the flake to embezzle money from needy children.

Many of the comic inversions of Hawks in *Lebowski* are structural or atmospheric rather than pinprick strikes on specific scenes. Above all, the standard joke about *The Big Sleep* – its bewildering, even

nonsensical over-complication – is played to great effect in *Lebowski*, where the first viewing might end in utter bafflement were it not for the fact that nothing of much significance turns out to have actually happened (apart from the embezzlement). The Dude keeps explaining that 'it's a complicated case', which is true in one sense, but ultimately the simplicity of the basic facts is disguised by the amount of overlapping characters all grasping pitifully for the same money.

Hawks's lush, rainy, dark, brooding and highly artificial *mise en scène*, constructed on sound stages, gives way to the Coens' reliance on a sunny if offbeat L.A., in which most of the locations are real: classic coffee shops and diners, the interiors of mansions and, of course, the classic 1950s Brunswick style of the bowling alley. 'Certainly we didn't want it to look like a noir,' Ethan told William Preston Robertson; quite the opposite, in fact.[52] In place of Hawks's fantastical nightscapes, *Lebowski* presents a real-life L.A. that isn't much seen in film. Just as the Dude is barely recognisable as the hardboiled hero of genre convention, the film's San Fernando Valley locations are not part of Los Angeles as conventionally recognised by the movies, or indeed by many Angelenos themselves.

The slobby, shambling Dude suits them as well as the impossibly sharp Marlowe suits Hawks's imagined version of the city proper. Instead of Bogart, immaculately dressed, never without the perfect wisecrack, magnetically attractive to any female who crosses his path, *Lebowski* offers the overweight, magnificently unkempt Jeff Bridges, dressed in cheap sunglasses, jelly shoes and a variety of clashing outfits sanded down by Mary Zophres to make them look appropriately dilapidated.[53] Whereas Marlowe throws out effortless witticisms under pressure – 'she tried to sit in my lap while I was still standing up'; 'you know what he'll do when he comes back? Beat my teeth out then kick me in the stomach for mumbling' – the Dude comes up with such gems as 'that's just, like, your opinion, man'. (To be fair to the Dude, he gets in the occasional decent crack, especially in the opening scene: 'Obviously, you're not a golfer.')

No woman can glance at Marlowe without giving him the eye; the Dude gets cold
stares and the solace of ridiculous fantasy

Marlowe, in David Thomson's apt description, is a man who always remains 'ahead of the game, always having the last witty remark, solving the infernal case and ending up, as it were, in sole possession', of the girl, the truth, the game, the case and the concept of manhood.[54] The Dude, meanwhile, has no idea why his landlord might be reminding him that it's the second week of the month and comes to such riveting investigative conclusions as 'new shit has come to light'. Of course, as Eddie Robson rightly notes, once the Dude comes to understand that the Big Lebowski doesn't really have any money of his own, he immediately solves the case according to the principles he had laid down in the bowling alley: look for the person who benefits.[55] But his detective work is usually atrocious. Even when he is convinced he is about to be killed by Bunny's kidnappers, his response is to return to his bungalow, where everyone knows he lives, and to get high in the bathtub. Not exactly a smooth operator, then – but the Dude *is* attuned to human psychology.

The Dude, like Marlowe (not to mention Chandler and Hawks), loves a drink, but his preference, the White Russian, feminises him with its hint of sugar and mother's milk. Chandler once described in a letter how much Marlowe hated these kinds of drinks: 'He will drink practically anything that is not sweet. Certain drinks, such as Pink Ladies, Honolulu cocktails and crème de menthe highballs, he would regard as an insult.'[56] The tightly controlled, scintillating battles of wit between Bogart and Bacall become the lame-brained ramblings of Bridges, who, in his extraordinarily paced deliveries, hardly ever finishes a sentence even when he's not being

How (not) to drink a cocktail

interrupted. The seduction at the heart of Hawks's *The Big Sleep*, its centrepiece of romance, becomes Maude's determination to shanghai the Dude into impregnating her. The sly femme fatale becomes a blunt, stuffy, stilted feminist artist who craves such complete control over her own destiny that she doesn't even want the father of her baby 'to be someone I have to see socially, or who'll have any interest in rearing the child himself'.

Although *Lebowski* is obviously a send-up of *The Big Sleep* in many ways, there is an intriguing sense in which the intentions of Hawks and the Coens are actually surprisingly similar. The great complication is that Hawks himself was making light of noir. By exaggerating the over-complicated nature of Chandler's already baroque narrative until it essentially falls to pieces, Hawks, David Thomson argues, is also more broadly 'making fun of plot'. And Hawks lacks the fatalism that remains the keynote of noir. '*The Big Sleep* looks and sometimes feels like a film noir, which – clearly – is a mistaken or much less than adequate labelling of the film,' writes Thomson. In fact, the film has transmogrified the novel into a love story, or what Thomson calls 'an exuberant mating ritual' between Bogart-Marlowe and Bacall-Vivian; hardly the grim doom of *Double Indemnity*, and most unlike a Chandler novel, which almost always insists on Marlowe's self-sufficiency and lack of entanglements or connections as a keynote of his heroic nature. In fact, Thomson goes so far as to label the film a send-up of Hollywood that presages later scepticism about narrative itself: '*The Big Sleep* inaugurates a post-modern, camp, satirical view of movies being about other movies that extends to the New Wave and *Pulp Fiction*.'[57]

It's easy to see *The Big Lebowski* as a logical progression or even a kind of culmination of this notion. This places the Coens as descendants of Hawks, not merely his satirists or imitators. They are teasing Hawks in the way that Hawks teased Chandler. The film is an exaggerated and extreme version of the 1990s retro/camp tendency, but it is more parodic and deliberately subversive. On this view, *The Big Lebowski* could be thought of as mock-noir in the playful Hawksian mode, although it entails far more explicit undermining, like *The Long Goodbye*. And yet for all that, the film still manages to convey the characteristic noir atmosphere of dreamlike disorientation, even if here it is addled rather than scary.

Leigh Brackett, who co-wrote the script of *The Big Sleep*, also co-wrote the script of *The Long Goodbye*. Even the great Chandler himself mocked the movie-making industry relentlessly in his novels and essays; at one point Marlowe describes how thugs now comport themselves 'as Hollywood has taught it should be done'.[58] The Coens, like Brackett, can do crime straight, or they can do it winking – but they can also do it laughing out loud. Like Hawks, and like Billy Wilder, they believe in laughter more fundamentally than they do in the supposed tenets of noir, although all of them can 'do' noir as a delightfully mannered *style*. For Hawks, according to Thomson, 'the whole thing is a game'.[59] Walter comes closest to grasping the Hawksian nature of the Lebowski case, with its myriad ins, outs and what-have-yous: 'it *is* a fucking game!'

3 What Makes a Man?

'Here is a man,' ran *Movie* magazine's retrospective celebration of Hawks.[60] Hawks's ideas about masculinity change little from picture to picture, and they are probably even more unbending than John Huston's, which is saying something. At least in *The Misfits* (1960), Huston faithfully presents Arthur Miller's notion that being a person might be even better than being a man. For Hawks, manliness essentially boils down to mastery, over one's environment, over one's tongue and especially over one's women. The sexual pecking orders in *The Big Sleep* and *His Girl Friday* are stunning to behold; Hawks's women must be feisty, witty and commanding, but in the end they often embrace happy enslavement to the right man. Compared with Dick Powell's Marlowe in *Murder, My Sweet* or Robert Montgomery's Marlowe in *Lady in the Lake*, the Marlowe created by Hawks and Bogart is more obviously in charge of absolutely everything and everyone. Nobody pushes him around, like the thugs do in the novels. Chandler, in fact, preferred Powell to Bogart, but he clearly wanted Marlowe to participate in the construction of masculinity characteristic of much early twentieth-century American literature, especially in Hemingway and Faulkner. The heroic tough guy – of course characteristic of the crime genre in general, including classic noir – was the early twentieth-century answer to the feminised Victorian values that many of these writers and film-makers believed had stifled American culture during the 1800s.[61]

The Big Lebowski, like a surprisingly large number of Coen films, meditates more or less constantly on the subject of masculinity, but it inverts the Hawksian conception of mastery at every turn. If the Coen oeuvre might be described as an extended frolic through the archives of film history, it is also a re-examination of the classic themes of 1940s Hollywood and, above all, the notion of what it means to be a man.

Having come of age as film-makers just after the Reagan years, it is unsurprising that the Coens tend to take up fake masculinity, phoney toughness and cowboy acting more than anything else. Like the 'Gipper', the era harked back to the conceptions of manhood formulated during Hollywood's Golden Age, with a new breed of self-sufficient over-achievers ruthless in their pursuit of capital and status – a model of manliness that tends towards *Wall Street*'s Gordon Gekko and, eventually, *American Psycho*'s Patrick Bateman. Yet throughout their work, the Coens have been sceptical of rugged individualism and its corollary, patronising chivalry.

In *Blood Simple*, both Ray (John Getz) and Marty (Dan Hedaya) are destroyed by their attempts to match up to norms of virility: the former's insecure machismo leads only to prolonged humiliation and fatal bitterness, while the latter's misplaced effort at 'being a gentleman' saddles him with the bloody burden that breaks him. Each, in his way, is a self-unmade man whose insecurity sets in train the events that consume him. *Raising Arizona* offers a comical but comparable instance of such proud self-harming, when Hi (Nicolas Cage) jeopardises his job by punching his foreman for suggesting wife-swapping. Hi's actions are unappreciated by his wife Ed (Holly Hunter):

ED   You're a grown man with responsibilities... Where does that leave the three of us? Where does that leave our entire family unit?

HI   With a man for a husband.

ED   That ain't no answer.

HI   Honey, that's the only answer.

ED   That ain't no answer.

HI   With a man for a husband.

Soon after, Hi justifies his return to armed robbery by noting in casually Reaganite terms that 'I come from a long line of frontiersmen and outdoor types' – an ironic echo of the President's 'Morning in America' campaign.

'We used the word "manly" a lot in reference to *Miller's Crossing*,' recalled cinematographer Barry Sonnenfeld.[62] Its characters set out to establish the most efficient means of asserting and maintaining power, pitching reason against instinct with ethics left to flounder somewhere in between. Tom Regan (Gabriel Byrne), a classic tough guy in the Dashiell Hammett mould, approaches self-sufficiency, if not nobility: always one step ahead, always in control, successful to a large degree in his attempts to remain above and apart from the messy business at hand, Regan still comes to learn that he can't control everything; and, what's more, that such mastery is a dubious ambition that distracts from 'the difficulty', in David Thomson's phrase, 'and nearly the shame, in admitting feeling'.[63]

Barton Fink has pretty much the opposite problem: a veneer of empathy that in fact papers over an emotional deafness. Barton must confront the fact that his passionate fellow-feeling is so much narcissistic blah, his affinity with 'the common man' quickly dissolving when that man is laughing too loudly next door or trying to have a dance in Barton's place. 'You're a real man,' he tells Charlie (John Goodman), the desperately sad psychopath whose stories he refuses to hear. Barton is a kind of anti-Tom Regan, a boy adrift in his own fantasies of masculinity, willing, for instance, to both indulge and judge his washed-up idol W. P. Mayhew without coming close to understanding him. 'If you were a man,' a 'Young Hussy' says in his wrestling screenplay, 'a real man, you'd slap me.'

Fargo also builds its narrative around competing notions of masculinity. Can it be coincidence that Mamet regular William H. Macy was cast as Jerry Lundegaard, the disastrous salesman who competes with his pack-leader father-in-law Wade (Harve Presnell) for control of 'the deal' that is his wife's staged kidnapping? Jerry's manhood is a deadpan Midwestern joke here, the awful gag being that he longs for the type of self-motivated efficacy with which Wade shrugs him off: his request for a loan is met with the dismissive 'I'm not talking about your damn *word*, Jerry' – a double slap that marks the proffered currency as both inappropriate and base. Meanwhile, the weedy Carl

Showalter (Steve Buscemi) has a combustible inferiority complex ('I guess you think you're, you know, like an authority figure in that stupid fucking uniform, huh, buddy?' he snaps at a parking attendant. 'King Clip-On Tie there, big fucking man, huh?'). His bullish refusal to forfeit his share of a family car costs him not only the $920,000 he's stashed away in the snow, but also his life.

In *O Brother, Where Art Thou?* Everett McGill (George Clooney) is chronically anxious about being unmanned while away from home, rightly perceiving his status as 'paterfamilias' and 'the king of this goddamn castle' to be threatened. *The Man Who Wasn't There* is no more or less than the excavation of a misanthropy so ingrained as to have passed through disdain into utter indifference; other characters are repeatedly moved to ask Ed, in consternation as well as anger, 'what kind of man *are* you?' When Miles Massey (Clooney) is bested by Marilyn Rexroth (Catherine Zeta Jones) in *Intolerable Cruelty*, his boss tells him to 'act like a man', while *The Ladykillers*' Mrs Munson (Irma P. Hall) appeals for guidance to the

Useless men (clockwise from top left): *Blood Simple*; *Barton Fink*; *O Brother, Where Art Thou?*; *Fargo*

memory of her beloved husband Othar, who was 'some kind of man' (almost an exact match for the phrase used to dubiously describe Welles's Hank Quinlan in 1958's *Touch of Evil*).

The Coens' *No Country for Old Men* – unreleased at the time of writing – is adapted from a Cormac McCarthy novel whose characters are consumed and often destroyed by the determination to act like 'real men'. Its climactic exchange sees the central character – a decorated Vietnam veteran – questioning his status as 'a war hero', considering whether his father was 'a better man' than himself and suggesting that he is 'not the man of an older time they say I am. I wish I was. I'm a man of this time.'[64] In each of their films, then, the Coens offer case studies in the pursuit of manliness as a hiding to nothing, a vain, shallow and frequently hypocritical exercise in hubris that leaves one at best embarrassed, at worst dead.

When America was The Man

The Big Lebowski, like *Blood Simple* and *Raising Arizona*, has characters who gesture specifically to Reaganite notions of individualistic accomplishment without help from the state or the outside world. The Big Lebowski is lost in the 1980s just as the Dude is lost in the 1960s. 'I suggest you do as your parents did, and get a job, sir!' screams the Big Lebowski, a loather of 'handouts' and 'bums'. But this phoney millionaire – who, we discover later on, has himself 'failed to achieve' at running the Lebowski companies – is not a follower of his own philosophy, any more than Reagan served in America's armed forces anywhere outside a sound stage. In light of this, it hardly seems accidental that *The Big Lebowski* shows news footage of Reagan's successor, George H. W. Bush, the 'wimp' scoffed at for going through the postures of the Gulf War as a kind of public muscle-building display. Ironically, of course, Bush Snr actually *was* a combat-hardened military hero. But his wan, stuttering, bespectacled threats about Saddam Hussein's 'unchecked aggression against Kuwait' aptly resonate throughout a film that in many ways is about losers pretending to be real men. Their inane posturing is thrown into relief by the thought that, across the ocean, others are genuinely putting their lives on the line for (what they at least perceive as) righteous causes: as Eddie Robson has noted, *The Big Lebowski* shares with *The Big Sleep* and Altman's Vietnam-era *The Long Goodbye* the setting of a Los Angeles far removed and isolated from a distant overseas war. Chandler himself had developed Marlowe against the backdrop of World War II prior to US engagement, publishing *Farewell, My Lovely* in 1940. Barton Fink too completes his first screenplay as Pearl Harbor is attacked.[65]

While the Coens' use of Saddam and a backdrop of war in Iraq might seem bizarrely prophetic in light of later events, it also carries a whiff of the fin-de-everything political and cultural atmosphere of late 1990s America. Saddam's remarkable endurance as both a national bugbear and a comedic butt, including the depiction of the tyrant as the Devil's homosexual lover in the feature *South Park: Bigger, Longer & Uncut* (1999), suggests the sort of limitless self-confidence that accompanied the high-water mark of American empire. Although some critics have attempted to read elaborate political symbolism into items such as the 'Heil Hitler!' Goodman's character gives at the climax of *Barton Fink*, it seems implausible to make much of such political references in *Lebowski*. That said, there is a certain suggestiveness to the use of the Gulf War as a framing device, as well as Walter's offhand anti-Arab racial slurs about 'fig eaters' and 'that camel-fucker in Iraq'. As a snapshot of a cultural moment, the entire story unfolds during a war of which the local squabble is a trivial, decadent and laughably meaningless shadow. The film also skewers the confused, endlessly self-referential culture of the post-Cold War period, the delusions of the End of History and the ideas of permanent American supremacy that helped induce the jaded, self-consuming feeling of the 1990s. Nearly ten years later, how different the world seems: *Lebowski* crystallises the instant when America was basically The Man.

The film's discrediting of traditional models of masculine authority begins with the Stranger's opening narration. Just as the

Western form – the generic equivalent of the man's man – is progressively compromised and bastardised until we're left with a lazy man drinking milk in a supermarket, the credibility of the narrator himself – conventionally the omniscient source of reliable information – collapses before our ears into the arch-inanity of 'Sometimes there's a man... Wal, I lost m' train of thought here...' More than this, the content of the Stranger's speech, so far as it's possible to discern, is a radical rejection of the very concept of heroism – 'what's a hee-ro?' – in favour of 'the man for his time 'n' place. He just fits right in there.' Rather than the exceptional character who stands against the tide of corruption or the noble iconoclast of the Great American West, we are asked to credit the reed that bends with the wind, the easy-going drifter, the tumbling tumbleweed. Certainly, the Dude is pretty hard to shock: think of the nonchalant, noncommital 'huh!' with which he greets his reflection in the Big Lebowski's *Time* magazine mirror, news of Quintana's pederasty or the sight of Maude's splatter-art. The Dude is also consistently averse to confrontation, opting out of aggressive situations by walking away or other means. During times of stress or impending violence – when Treehorn's thugs shove his head down the toilet or the Big Lebowski rants at him on their first meeting – the Dude simply puts his shades on.

These two early confrontations establish the Dude as uninterested in competing with either macho or materialist conceptions of manliness. Treehorn's goons, with their well-coiffed hair and ripped biceps, seem to represent a porn version of masculinity; it would hardly be surprising if they performed for Treehorn on camera as well as enforcing for him. Their presence calls to mind the hired muscle of Marty Augustine (Mark Rydell) in *The Long Goodbye* – ersatz versions of sex and violence for hire, potency by the pound designed to flatter the male consumer's delusions of mastery. Augustine literally has his men – including future Governor Schwarzenegger – strip to illustrate his puissance. 'That's why they sent me,' Uli-as-Karl-as-the Cable Guy drawls in *Logjammin'*, slamming the television as a prelude

to sexual intercourse, 'I am an expert.' Bunny's hydrophilic co-star (played by real-life porn star Asia Carrera) cannot control herself once exposed to this stud's charms: 'You must be here to fix the cable.' What could be hotter? Not long after, Jesus Quintana offers a similarly preening, oversexed attempt at dominance. (It's probably just as well that the outsized false phallus visible in his pants during the brief flashback sequences wasn't used in his bowling suit; costume designer Mary Zophres has suggested this might have landed the film with an NC-17 rating.[66]) The Dude is as unmoved by Quintana's sexualised playground taunts – all 'fuck you' this and 'in the ass' that – as he is by the cockiness of Treehorn's thugs.[67]

Hello, boys: Marty Augustine and Jackie Treehorn get some help in

The Big Lebowski, meanwhile, conforms to another ostentatiously self-aggrandising type familiar from other Coen films: like Marty in *Blood Simple*, Nathan Arizona and *Barton Fink*'s Jack Lipnik, he goes to considerable lengths to display the trophies of his accomplishments, 'the various commendations, honorary degrees, citations of merit, et cetera' that Brandt insists the Dude examine (but not touch). 'Achiever' is the key word here, mentioned on no fewer than four of the Big Lebowski's plaques and mementoes, and the concept of success for which it stands seems to be characterised by self-sufficiency and a concomitant refusal to take responsibility for anyone else:

I hope that someday my wife will learn to live on her allowance, which is ample, but if she does not, that is *her* problem, not mine, just as the rug is *your* problem, just as every bum's lot in life is his own responsibility regardless of who he chooses to blame. I didn't blame anyone for the loss of my legs – some Chinaman took them from me in Korea, but I went out and achieved anyway.

'Bums' occupy an especially demonised position in this worldview, partly for being a perceived drain on others' resources – like the 'welfare queens' whom Reagan accused of draining the American

'Please, feel free to inspect them'

lifeblood – no matter that the Big Lebowski himself turns out to be entirely dependent on others. One senses that his namesake irritates him particularly, perhaps as a form of a double or mirror image of himself, one that dares to reject the very terms on which this definition of achievement rests. Certainly, the Dude is utterly unmoved by the Big Lebowski's trophies and trappings – and, perhaps more remarkably, by his wealth itself.[68] During the Dude's second visit to the Lebowski mansion, when the old man is in highly theatrical 'seclusion' in his great-room, the Big Lebowski's pompous, combative conception of manhood is explicitly laid out, and equally explicitly contrasted with the Dude's utter lack of interest in engaging with – let alone proving himself worthy of – any such type. In a brilliant bit of business played with the perfection of vocal pitch and timing characteristic of Jeff Bridges throughout the film, the Dude seems to be picking something out of his teeth as Lebowski holds forth – perhaps a stray bit of weed?

BIG LEBOWSKI   Funny. I can look back on a life of achievement, challenges
                met, competitors bested, obstacles overcome. I've
                accomplished more than most men, and without the use of
                my legs. What – What makes a man, Mr Lebowski?

DUDE   Dude.

BIG LEBOWSKI   ...eh?

DUDE   Ah, I, I don't know, sir.

BIG LEBOWSKI   Is it being prepared to do the right thing, whatever the cost? Isn't that what makes a man?

DUDE   Mm, sure, that and a pair of testicles.

BIG LEBOWSKI   Joking. But perhaps you're right...

DUDE   You mind if I do a jay?

The DUDE takes a joint out of his pocket.

BIG LEBOWSKI   Bunny...

DUDE   'Scuse me?

BIG LEBOWSKI   Bunny Lebowski. She is the light of my life. Are you surprised at my tears, sir?

The DUDE, who has been concentrating on sparking up, redirects his attention.

DUDE   Oh, fuckin' A.

BIG LEBOWSKI   Strong men also cry. Strong men also cry... I received this fax this morning.

BRANDT shows the DUDE the fax, which he reads while BIG LEBOWSKI continues speaking.

BIG LEBOWSKI   As you can see, it is a ransom note, written by men who are unable to achieve on a level field of play. Cowards! Weaklings! Bums!

Suspicious from the start (although the Dude doesn't seem to catch on), Lebowski's portentous pontificating is also scripted, if Brandt's antic fist-clenching and rictus grin are anything to go by. Lebowksi's words assume a ludicrous dramatic irony once we learn that far from 'being prepared to do the right thing' and struggling 'to achieve on a level field of play', he owes his standing to his dead first wife's family and is speaking as part of a plan to defraud a children's charity.

One of the boys

Lebowski expects the Dude to be cowed by the scene he has constructed, but as usual he barely acknowledges his surroundings; as Joel has noted, 'the Dude tends to get into spaces and get pretty comfortable pretty fast'.[69] In fact, his body language is remarkably open in almost all circumstances, including those in which he would

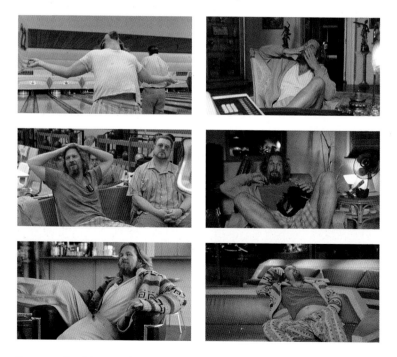

Pretty comfortable pretty fast

do well to be wary, such as at Jackie Treehorn's pad or during the invasion of his own home. The Dude likes to put his legs up. This characteristic, richly expressive of the Dude's general indifference to social status, is likely to have been considered from the earliest stages of pre-production. 'We've often discussed with [storyboard artist] J. Todd [Anderson] how posture is everything,' Joel has recalled. 'How a character carries himself physically. It's an important thing and it often gets expressed in the storyboards.'[70] Bridges has perfected the Dude's slouching posture and constant state of facial befuddlement much as Bogart perfected Marlowe's observant readiness.

The Dude's openness suggests an ease not necessarily shared by the other male characters, who often indulge in conspicuously hyper-masculine posturing. Note, for example, the way the Chief of Police of Malibu makes the effort to put on his hat before assaulting the Dude, a tic shared by several other Coen characters: Visser in *Blood Simple*, Tom in *Miller's Crossing* and Grimsrud in *Fargo* all don headgear before engaging in combat. By contrast, the Dude's exposure of his oh-so-soft underbelly would seem to leave him open to the threat of castration laced none too subtly throughout the film, most conspicuously in Maude's scissor paintings and the nihilists'

'Stay out of Malibu, deadbeat!' (Note the trophy wall)

explicit threat to chop off his 'Johnson' (and maybe 'skvush' it). Although he's understandably keen to hold on to that all-important 'pair of testicles', the Dude's nonchalant conception of 'man' as a mere biological category rather than an ethically loaded identity points to a suggestion that runs throughout *The Big Lebowski*, and indeed the Coens' work in general: that real men are in fact women. Or, to put it another way, while the men bluster around trying to prove themselves worthy of the name, it's the female characters who thrive and get things done, adopting conventionally 'manly' behaviour as the occasion demands.

In *Blood Simple*, for instance, Abby's (Frances McDormand) simple common sense is enough to make her the last person standing, while in *Raising Arizona* it's the female member of the central couple, a uniformed police officer called Ed, who sets the agenda – a fact noted by Gale when he provocatively asks her husband 'who wears the pants around here'. Male characters are often subtly emasculated in such ways, as in the scene in *The Man Who Wasn't There* in which Ed Crane shaves his wife's legs while she bathes and smokes. By the end of *Miller's Crossing*, Tom is no better off than at the start, but Verna (Marcia Gay Harden) has brought about the match she wanted. 'The funny thing is,' boss Leo (Albert Finney) bashfully admits to Regan, 'she asked me to tie the knot. I guess you're not supposed to say that.' In *Barton Fink*, Audrey (Judy Davis) appears to be the only character actually capable of producing creative work; it seems she's so powerful that after her death her severed head serves as Barton's muse. In *The Hudsucker Proxy*, Norville (Tim Robbins) has Amy Archer (Jennifer Jason Leigh) pretty accurately pegged as 'one of those fast-talking career gals [who] thinks she's one of the boys. Probably is one of the boys, if you know what I mean... Probably dresses in men's clothing, swaps drinks with the guys at the local watering hole, hobnobs with some smooth-talking heel in the newsroom...' Here, the attempt to out-man the men is seen to do Amy no favours; she is so successful in her campaign that it undermines her self-esteem.

Fargo's Marge Gunderson, on the other hand, achieves maximum efficacy without any apparent detriment to her status as wife and mother-to-be; instead of occupying a conventionally supplicant female role, as Frances McDormand has noted, 'the men in her life are defined by her'.[71] *Intolerable Cruelty* and *The Ladykillers* are both stories of women overcoming male presumption, albeit of different kinds.

Like Jerry Lundegaard before him and *The Man Who Wasn't There*'s Big Dave (James Gandolfini) after him, the Big Lebowski is a sort of trophy husband, dependent on his first wife's capital for his own comfortable status. 'The wealth was all mother's,' Maude reveals. 'We did let [father] run one of the companies briefly but he didn't do very well at it. No, he helps administer the charities now and I give him a reasonable allowance. He has no money of his own.' The *real* Big Lebowski, in other words, was Maude's mother, who even appears to have disinherited her husband; following her death 'He has no money of his own'. The great lengths to which he goes to project an image of worldly masculinity are plainly rooted in a profound sense of inadequacy; in the screenplay, the climactic scene in which Walter lifts him out of his wheelchair concludes with an exchange that didn't make it to the screen. 'Stay away from me, you

Raising Arizona's Ed, wearing pants

bullies!' the Big Lebowski blubs, still sprawled on the floor. 'You and these women! You won't leave a man his fucking balls!' (That pair of testicles again...)

Perhaps the most radical emasculation the Coens propose, however, is not mere castration but rather the co-option of a man's balls by a more potent woman. The Dude here, like Everett McGill in *O Brother, Where Art Thou?*, is reduced to the status of sperm donor, good for procreation and nothing else. The coldly efficient – not to mention unilateral – fashion in which Maude obtains the Dude's stud services is the very antithesis of romance, but utterly typical of her status as the film's real pack leader. Alone among the characters, she knows what she wants and gets it, as well as taking responsibility for the Lebowski family name and the Urban Achievers. The metaphor is literalised in the 'opening credits' of the Dude's drugged-out dream sequence, when a pair of bowling balls and a pin are set up to resemble male genitalia before being demolished. But even in his fantasies, the best the Dude can do is administer a bowling lesson to a strong woman with very big horns, and indulge in a little wide-eyed scopophilia.

Amateurs, bums and sex offenders

In stark contrast to the Dude's avoidance of conflict is Walter's line-in-the-sand mentality of picking fights over the broaching of more or less arbitrary boundaries and working himself up into apoplexy simply to prove his intransigence. 'Over the line!' he bellows at Smokey (Jimmie Dale Gilmore) over a perceived foul. 'This is not 'Nam, this is bowling. There are rules!'. Having pulled his gun, he demonstrates his constitutional inability to back down from a confrontation, screaming as he breaks Lord knows how many federal laws: 'AM I THE ONLY ONE WHO GIVES A SHIT ABOUT THE RULES?' This exchange perfectly exemplifies the curious tension in Walter's personality between a demand for structure and a wrathful incontinence. In many ways, his faith in brute force ('I grab one of 'em and beat it out of him') and ferocity in combat (biting the lead nihilist's ear off) verge on the bestial. His substitution of his 'whites' for the Big Lebowski's ransom bag is an exercise in alpha-male face-rubbing only one step away from the rug-pissers' territory-marking.

Walter, in other words, is not quite housebroken. This might go some way to explaining his need for rules and regulations: he may not know what kind of dog Cynthia owns, but he knows that it has 'papers', which presumably is more important than knowing what is

'There are rules!'

actually written on them. This need is most evident in Walter's dependency on institutionalised hierarchies, from his long-completed military service to his dissolved marriage, from league bowling to his highly dubious version of Judaism. These notions of framing and naming come together when the pederast bowler, Jesus Quintana, confronts Walter, the Dude and Donny about moving their bowling showdown from Saturday to Wednesday in order to accommodate the Jewish Sabbath. This already hilarious scene is made more so because it is an obscene parody of the New Testament:

What's this 'day of rest' shit? What's this bullshit? I don't fucking care! It don't matter to Jesus!... I would've fucked you in the ass Saturday. I'll fuck you in the ass next Wednesday instead! Wooo! You got a date Wednesday, baby!

This, of course, echoes Jesus's argument against the Pharisees for their over-scrupulous observance of religious boundaries, as in the Gospel of Luke when they accuse Jesus of healing the sick on the Sabbath. The film sets Walter up as a comic Pharisee, since his put-on Jewish identity seems to be more about stiffly following a strictly regulated life than any deep and loving communion with God, his synagogue or other Jews – even if the weekend activities this Jesus has to offer the world are slightly more secular. Walter's woeful notion of being Jewish is not only a part of his 'sick Cynthia thing' (he converted before his now-dissolved marriage), but also seems like a logical replacement for the regimentation of his much-missed army life – a far cry, to put it mildly, from what any rabbi would teach.

For Walter, manhood requires a codified ethical framework to which action is accountable, the ability to successfully channel one's urges into such a structure being a characteristic of the successful man, hence his pedantic pride in the case-law of the First Amendment ('the Supreme Court has roundly rejected prior restraint!') and his shock at learning that the Germans are not Nazis but nihilists. It's nearly the only moment where we see him lost for words, a haunted look marking his features.[72] 'Fuck me,' he eventually exhales.

'I mean, say what you want about the tenets of National Socialism, Dude, at least it's an ethos.' Similarly, despite his rejection of Smokey's pacifism as 'not something to hide behind', he makes a fleeting attempt at refuge behind the universally recognised two-fingered 'peace' sign when set upon by the Sellers' neighbour, whose Corvette he was pummelling with a crowbar seconds before.

Such a worldview also accounts for Walter's perennial disdain for 'amateurs', those incapable of fulfilling the tasks they have set themselves. 'Amateurs' are to Walter as 'bums' are to the Big Lebowski – the flip-side to his fruitless search for a 'worthy fuckin' adversary' and fuel for his persecution complex. It comes as no surprise that Walter so loves *Branded*, the 1965–6 NBC TV show set in the old West in which a US cavalry captain – sole survivor of an Indian massacre, unjustly discharged for cowardice – roams the land trying to do good and clear his name, whatever others think of him. Although the series' supposed creator, Arthur Digby Sellers (Harry Bugin), is fictional and the number of episodes is exaggerated in the film, the show was real. Its transmission coincided with the entrenchment of the Vietnam War, and evidently struck a chord with militaristic young Walter. It must have resonated with him after the war, too, if his service earned him no respect back home. The lyrics to

Walter sues for peace

the theme song suggest why he might have found it 'truly a source of inspiration':

All but one man died there at Bitter Creek
And they say he ran away.
Branded! Scorned as the one who ran.
What do you do when you're branded and you know you're a man?
Wherever you go for the rest of your life you must prove you're a man.

Proof is key to Walter's view of his own manhood: if asked (and, more frequently, even if not asked), he volunteers a vehemently held argument in support of any of his jackass tactics and opinions; he insists on the last word and would much rather be right than liked. When the Dude tells him 'you're not wrong, Walter, you're just an asshole', there's no reason to think Walter objects to the assessment. Although he retains an obvious albeit well-hidden love for the Dude and Donny, his interaction with them is defined by one question ('Am I wrong?') and one abusive conversation killer ('Shut the fuck up, Donny').

A social history of dudeness

Plainly, the Dude is of a different disposition, one that leaves him open to being taken for a sap now and then. His rather mild reaction to having his home invaded by the nihilists – 'this is a private residence, man', as if there were some simple confusion that might be cleared up easily – suggests that the Dude's home is not really his castle. 'Now "Dude",' the Stranger mulls in his introduction. 'That's a name no one would self-apply where I come from...' The fact that 'Dude' is a proudly worn badge of identity rather than an imposed label of belittlement or shame is one of the earliest signs that we're not in the Wild West after all, but in more-or-less contemporary California. Having come into circulation in the 1870s – around the time of *Branded*'s setting – to denote a man conspicuously concerned with look and dress, in pioneer country 'dude' had pejorative connotations of effeteness, incompetence or unfitness. The 'dude' was the opposite of the manly hero, the outsider, often from back East or the city, incapable of dealing with the rough real-world situation.

Cinematically speaking, this kind of dudeness was one of the earliest forms of clownery: 1898's *Some Dudes Can Fight* and the 1903 Edison silent comedies *The Dude and the Bootblacks* and *The Dude and the Burglars* offered a dandified butt. The tradition continued with the comic short *The Dude Cowboy* (1912) and on to *The Dude Ranger* (1934), about an Easterner who inherits a ranch. The idea of the 'dude ranch' – a resort version of the West catering for city-slicker tourists – informed Disney's 1951 short 'Dude Duck', which cast Donald Duck as a vacationer. Dean Martin's drunk was called the Dude in *Rio Bravo* (1959) and Lee Marvin spits the term at Jimmy Stewart throughout *The Man Who Shot Liberty Valance* (1962). Such regrettable associations reached as far as Hull and Philip Larkin's *The Whitsun Weddings* (1964), in which the speaker of 'A Study of Reading Habits' bitterly notes his own resemblance to 'the dude/Who lets the girl down before/The hero arrives'. In this context, it is indeed a name few would self-apply.

By the late 1960s, however, the term had taken on another meaning, a cordial, even affectionate surfer slang usage. According to Ron Rosenbaum's playful excavation of the term, this process of reclamation drew upon the qualities of civility and gentlemanliness implicit in the word prior to its adoption as an ironic insult.[73] When, in *Easy Rider* (1969), George Hanson asks 'What's "dude"? Is that like "dude ranch"?', Captain America explains that '"Dude" means "nice guy". "Dude" means "a regular sort of person".' This could well have been the era when Jeffrey Lebowski formally assumed the title. (In an exchange from the screenplay that didn't make it into the movie, the Chief of Police of Malibu asks whether the Dude is 'some kind of sad-assed refugee from the fucking sixties', to which he replies 'Uh-huh'.) By the 1980s, this use of 'dude' was established in American popular culture, thanks to films like *Fast Times at Ridgemont High* (1982): as Scott Kiesling notes in his article on the word in *American Speech*, Sean Penn's Jeff Spicoli was an iconic 'dude'-using character, emblematic of the no-sweat, nothing-to-prove attitude embodied in the term: 'While he is clueless and often falls on hard times, Spicoli is consistently laid back, even in exasperation, and especially in encounters with authority.'[74] The same could be said of the lead in *Ferris Bueller's Day Off* (1986), of whom we are told 'the sportos, the motorheads, geeks, sluts, bloods, waistoids, dweebies, dickheads – they all adore him. They think he's a righteous dude.' Over the next few years, movies like *Bill and Ted's Excellent Adventure* (1989) and *Wayne's World* (1992), along with animated TV shows such as *Teenage Mutant Ninja Turtles* (1987–96) and *The Simpsons*, enshrined its use as emblematic of affably airheaded, nonconformist youth culture. By the end of the century it was restored to headline status in *Dude, Where's My Car?* (2000).

The 'dude' type, then, is established in firm counterpoint to that hard-headed, egotistical pursuer of capital and status, Reaganite man. Dudeness is a way of being a man that privileges sociability over industry and civility over self-furtherment. It is a fundamentally good-natured mode. Kiesling identifies it as a signifier of 'the small zone of "safe" solidarity between camaraderie and intimacy' that male friends can occupy without raising eyebrows; a term of endearment, in other words, an expression of a love that need not speak its name. From such a perspective, 'man' is less a mode to strive after than an all-purpose form of address, applicable to anyone and everyone from a fifteen-year-old boy to a chief of police. (The Dude adopts this usage well over a hundred times during the course of the film.) Such are the cultural vagaries of the terminology of American manhood; in the parlance of our times, and for good historical reasons, a young African-American male is a 'little man' rather than a 'boy', whereas a white male would rather be known as 'a dude' than 'the man' (except in jest).

This is not to say that our own Dude has no ego. He has a tendency to refer to himself in the third person, and shows a hint of nonchalant pride when telling Maude and Brandt about his 1960s activism. Nor does it mean that he is altogether lacking in the attributes becoming to a conventional man's man: he angrily confronts Da Fino when he feels Maude's safety is in question ('Stay away from my fucking lady friend, man!'), and when it comes down to it, he sticks his neck out for justice. Rather, it's that he has rejected conventional codes of masculinity in favour of his own terms, except for a camp appreciation of their surfaces. 'I dig your style too,' he tells the Stranger, good-naturedly deflecting what could have been seen as a pass, 'got a whole cowboy thing goin' on.' As the film's signature track by Bob Dylan has it, 'The man in me will hide sometimes to keep from being seen/But that's just because he doesn't want to turn into some machine.' In the Big Lebowski's mind, this nonconformism makes the Dude a bum, but there's little doubt which of them is better equipped to deal with outrageous fortune, the 'strikes and gutters, ups and downs' that constitute life as it's lived. Even in the old West context, a dude's outsider status could be a boon. The Allied Artists comedy *The Dude Goes West* (1948) concerns an intellectual Easterner who, in between pratfalls, offers some salient probing into the normative conceptions of women, Indians and bad guys. The Dude might be 'the wrong man' in more ways than one, but he isn't a phoney, and that makes him nigh-on unique in his world. Excused from the tiring, vain, arbitrary business of being a man, he can concentrate instead on being human.

4 The Religion of Laughter

Critics and audiences who dislike the Coen brothers persistently complain that their films lack heart and soul, are devoid of empathy, have generally unsympathetic characters and are too much in love with their own technical pyrotechnics and witticisms to give audiences anything to care about deeply. As Eddie Robson notes, the Coens have often been called aloof or elitist film-makers who condescend to their characters with broad regional stereotypes, especially vis-à-vis *Raising Arizona* and *Fargo*.[75] To a detractor, *The Big Lebowski* must have seemed like a crystallisation of all of these annoyances. Todd McCarthy remarked, in the 20 January 1998 edition of *Variety*, that 'the film doesn't seem to be about anything other than its own cleverness'. In the UK, the *Evening Standard*'s Alexander Walker similarly commented on 23 April that the Coens 'have let their fondness for pastiche run away with them to the extent that they're pastiching themselves'.[76]

The general line on *Lebowski*, even among those more sympathetic to the film, like Roger Ebert, was that it was no *Fargo*. *Fargo*, with its critical success and Academy Award recognition, had set a rather high bar. It was a spare, moody and evocative film whose barren Midwestern landscapes could give a person chills, a tone that would hardly have prepared an audience for the exuberant film history jukebox and vulgarian verbal onslaught that is *Lebowski*. The reversal of the production sequence for *Fargo* and *Lebowski*, which was caused by contingency, not deliberation, might have also thrown some for a loop. Even though *Lebowski* was well into production before *Fargo* fever struck the mainstream, it might have seemed as if the Coens were rejecting their newfound success by pushing audiences away with a film that even diehard fans found difficult to absorb on first viewing. Another commonplace among *Lebowski* commentators, including

Janet Maslin of *The New York Times* and Ian Nathan of *Empire*, was
that it would appeal only to audiences who cared about the Coens
already. Congenial bafflement was also widespread, with many critics
commending the film as enjoyable but beyond – or beneath –
constructive discussion.[77] At the US box office, the film grossed $17.5
million, about $7 million less than *Fargo*.

J. Hoberman of *The Village Voice* and Geoff Andrew of *Time Out*
were ahead of the curve in recognising that the film actually went out of
its way to upset the perception of coldness that has dogged the Coens'
film-making careers. Hoberman appreciated the fact that both *Fargo*
and *Lebowski* had 'affable' main characters, and put a pertinent
question: 'Have the Coens gone feel-good?' Of course, *Raising Arizona*
and *The Hudsucker Proxy* both had, like *Lebowski*, an endearingly
idiotic protagonist, but at least Hoberman was able to skim off the
incessantly abusive dialogue to see what was really underneath: the
Dude, Walter and Donny are ordinary people who like life and
genuinely care about each other, even though they spend most of their
time making a game of disguising their feelings by bickering and
insulting each other, pressing each others' buttons and acting out the
roles of a fractious family. 'I hate you – but call me,' in the words of the
Monks song playing when Walter pulls his piece at the lanes. Andrew

A fractious family?

was spot-on about the Coens' real intentions in *Lebowski*. 'Far from being shallow pastiche,' he wrote, 'it's actually about something: what it means to be a man, to be a friend, and to be a "hero" for a particular time and place'.[78]

Negative of a negative

Andrew's comment is particularly suggestive insofar as it implies, correctly and paradoxically, that the film actually takes seriously all of the themes that it mocks – an implication upon which Andrew expanded in his 1998 book *Stranger Than Paradise*, whose chapter on the Coens notes that such *outré* touches as the Stranger's prologue 'are not wacky red herrings but pertinent to the film as a whole'.[79] In *Lebowski*, all the ironic reversals of the crime genre appear to undertake a complicated double-flip. The satire hollows out the artificiality of the detective genre but the end result, oddly, is not a cynical, echoing shell. Instead, *Lebowski* places an ordinary person in the position of the hero, and then leaves an oddly optimistic view of life in place. This situates the film in the mode of classic literary comedy, which from Shakespeare to Laurence Sterne and Twain on down is designed to highlight human folly without by any means giving up on humanity.[80] *Lebowski* is a bit like a Shakespeare comedy, if only in the light-hearted sense that it celebrates life and love, ultimately endorsing marriage and ending with nuptials or sexual reproduction: in the end, Walter and the Dude embrace and go bowling, restoring equilibrium to their strange bachelor relationship. Meanwhile, the Stranger, now acting like a campy and anachronistic Epilogue in an old-fashioned closet drama, informs us that 'there's a little Lebowski on the way'. At any rate, Ethan's claim that *Lebowski* is a 'happy movie' is not a throwaway remark.[81] The notion of a 'religion of laughter', first applied to Sterne's eighteenth-century satire *Tristram Shandy*, could be used to describe the Coens' purpose in *Lebowski*: the classic convention-shredding anti-novel meets a gem of post-postmodern anti-film, both works finally and resolutely humanistic for all their put-ons and vulgarity.

The Coens had a far less remote source than classic literature, however, for their decision to make comedy the increasingly obvious basis of their film-making in the 1990s. The idiosyncratic Preston Sturges, frequently acknowledged as a major influence on the Coens, put forward a kind of artistic manifesto in favour of comedy in *Sullivan's Travels*. Sullivan is a movie producer whose life's ambition is to adapt the Depression-era epic *Oh Brother, Where Art Thou?* for the screen, in order to help his fellow man by bringing audiences to tears and inducing a feeling of universal human fellowship with the suffering of man.[82] Sullivan disguises himself as a hobo and goes on the road, only to wind up accidentally at a prison farm. His moment of revelation comes when the convicts are invited by a local church to watch some animated cartoons, and the uproarious laughter that fills the place of worship binds together all the different strata of society. In that moment, Sullivan decides to make comedies instead: laughter is itself a feeling of universal human fellowship. Helping out your fellow man means making them laugh for a while so that they can forget their troubles. It's the kinder thing to do.

Of course, there are many different kinds of laughter: the cruel laughter of bullies; the jibes and digs of enemies; the bubble-bursting of vanity, puffery and pretension (what Laurence Sterne called 'false

'A happy movie'

gravity' in *Tristram Shandy*); the kind of absurd or ludicrous play with language heard in works like *Alice in Wonderland*; the gracious self-mockery that falls into the category of 'what fools these mortals be'. One can laugh at human stupidity either from the perspective of condescension (the feeling engendered by Maude and Knox Harrington's fit of the giggles or the car-pound cop's sarcastic mention of 'the boys down at the crime lab'), or else with the humbling knowledge in mind that everybody plays the fool sometimes.[83] If one considers *Lebowski* alongside *Raising Arizona*, *The Hudsucker Proxy*, the neo-Sturges musical epic *O Brother, Where Art Thou?* and parts of the uneven *Intolerable Cruelty*, it seems clear that the Coen brand of humour is generally of the second, more cosmic, humane sort. *Blood Simple*, *Fargo*, *Miller's Crossing* and *The Man Who Wasn't There* are more dead-eyed and black-humoured, but these are films about confirmed outsiders. The Coen comic universe is largely populated by sweet, dumb goofballs who get themselves tangled up in trouble and are generally saved by external forces, or sometimes just coincidence. William Preston Robertson put it aptly in his summary of the Coens:

Their shared sense of humor is an impossible mix of offbeat, free-range intellectualism, slapstick of both the physical and metaphysical type, extremely subtle irony, extremely obvious irony, idiotic repetitive wordplay... Cerebral one minute, slaphappy the next, [Coen films] are set in a chaotic yet predetermined universe. Their movies are Postmodern Tales of Everyman exploring the proposition that we are all more or less imbeciles at one time or another... But the manner in which the chaos is presented is as precise and clean and certain as that in any movie made during Hollywood's Golden Age.[84]

Of course, the Coens have done even more than this, and it is their enormous range, both stylistic and emotional, that makes them more remarkable film-makers than many of their contemporaries. In what we might call their crime films – *Blood Simple*, *Miller's Crossing*, *Fargo*, *The Big Lebowski*, *The Man Who Wasn't There* and *The*

Ladykillers – they have shown a brilliant penchant for displaying every ugly variation of the banality of evil as well as an insistence on *Grand Guignol* splatter. And of course these films also have their own darker laughter that undercuts the seriousness with which their characters take themselves.

Robertson's more happy-go-lucky description of the Coen aesthetic suits *Lebowski*, a film which despite its crime genre appearances and film history pedigree is really a relatively pure comedy. As Eddie Robson points out, *Lebowski* was the Coens' 'least bloody film to date'.[85] The kidnapping is not even bogus so much as nonexistent; the solution to the great complex mystery of the film is that 'she didn't even kidnap herself'. No murders take place and the only real violence – always associated with the nihilists, strangers to fellow-feeling and *joie de vivre* – is self-inflicted (the girl sacrifices her toe to the phoney kidnapping ploy), ridiculous (Uli has his ear bitten off and spat into the air by Walter) or accidental (Donny's heart attack during the climactic parking-lot confrontation). Throughout that last scene, Walter, who has been verbally abusing Donny throughout the entire film, reveals a deeper level of feeling for his friend at the moment it matters most. Rather than telling him to shut up, he seems to comprehend the gravity of the situation in Donny's mind and rather wonderfully and empathetically rises to the occasion, telling him the Germans are nothing to be afraid of. 'They won't hurt us, Donny,' he says. 'These men are cowards.' It is the one moment when Walter's ridiculously inappropriate tough-guy antics and Vietnam combat flashbacks are of any use to his friends or himself. It fits very well with the overall tone of the film, and with the worldview of the Coen comedies, that Walter would turn out to be a muddled, oafish softie beneath his belligerent, unbalanced exterior – a fact even better revealed in the scene towards the end of the movie in which he botches the scattering of Donny's ashes. Goodman's way of flashing out a mercurial range of quickly changing but always heated emotions – simmering and boiling over – is ideal for making Walter both pathetic and at times bizarrely endearing.

Walter's finest hour

In praise of harmless idiots

If *Lebowski*, like many other Coen films, might be said to describe a struggle between the harmless idiots and the harmful idiots of this world, the Big Lebowski is downright toxic. Out of vanity, he takes a child-bride, but when Bunny begins to bore him, he (presumably) cuts her allowance and secretly hopes that she will be killed by the people he thinks have kidnapped her, so that he can embezzle $1 million from a children's charity. Human beings don't come a lot worse, although like Jerry Lundegaard, the Big Lebowski is entirely pathetic and banal. 'The other Jeffrey Lebowski, the millionaire,' is not even a millionaire.

The Dude's brain might be made of Swiss cheese, but he is notably considerate of others' well-being. One of the things he consistently remembers is information about children who are in trouble or need help. Even though she wants to raise the child herself, Maude is right that the Dude at least has the emotional makings of a good dad. Larry Sellers might be a joyriding little brat who (the Dude thinks) stole $1 million from the trunk of his car, but he also tells Jackie Treehorn that the kid is having difficulties in his social studies class, referring to the grade Larry received on his homework assignment about the Louisiana Purchase. Similarly, the Little Lebowski Urban Achievers stick in the Dude's mind, even though he has only seen a single picture of them on the Big Lebowski's trophy wall: he mentions them again to Maude, and from Walter's insulting comments to the Big Lebowski about stealing from 'needy little Urban Achievers' near the end of the film one might infer that the Dude has been harping on about the subject to his friend.

The Dude, in contrast to his namesake, never really cared about the money. His reaction to what he thinks is its disappearance is telling, and how remarkably unlike most other human beings it makes him is worth noting. There is something heroic, after all, about his attitude towards money. 'I was feeling really shitty earlier in the day,' he tells Tony (Dom Irrera), his limo driver. 'I'd lost a little money, I was down in the dumps... Fuck it! I can't be worrying

about that shit. Life goes on!' Don't forget that we're talking about
$1 million here – but hey, who cares? It was Walter's crack-brained
scheme to try to take the money in the first place. The Dude is so
lackadaisical about the briefcase – parking in the handicapped spot
at the bowling alley with the money in the trunk and, even more
oddly, not bothering to open the briefcase to see what $1 million
looks like – that his attitude towards its apparent loss seems
sincere.[86] The Dude doesn't really want that kind of money. One
senses that it's somehow against his principles. He's not joking
around when he says that all he ever wanted was his rug back – and
he says it right after sympathising with the kid who he thinks stole
his million, suggesting that all Larry Sellers wanted was a car.[87]

The Dude is sometimes unaware of even the most basic details
of the world around him. Even after their visit to shake down Larry
Sellers, he still believes Larry has the money and still associates him
with the Corvette we know belongs to the Sellers' neighbour. But he
gets psychology; as Nathan Arizona puts it in *Raising Arizona*, 'I
don't know much, but I know human beings.' As soon as the Dude
realises that the Big Lebowski has no money of his own and that his
business activities have been reduced to administering the Lebowski
family charities, he immediately grasps the entire case. While the

'I can't be worrying about that shit'

Dude is obviously disgusted that the Big Lebowski has manipulated him and intends to accuse him of the theft of the money, he is also disgusted by the embezzlement from the kids that Brandt had earlier called 'Mr Lebowski's children'. The Big Lebowski's phoniness is so extreme that Walter takes the extra step of assuming that his disability is also a put-on, resulting in his physical humiliation on the floor of his mansion.

The Dude's summation of the Big Lebowski as a 'human paraquat' encapsulates his entire worldview in two words, an oddly eloquent and strange description of everything he opposes in life. Paraquat is a toxic herbicide which was promoted by the United States in Mexico to destroy fields of marijuana. Its use was carefully circumscribed in the United States because of its health effects, but not south of the border. Smokers who used paraquat-coated marijuana sometimes complained of pulmonary fibrosis or 'paraquat lung', leading some to allege a deliberate conspiracy against dope smokers – a theory to which the Dude would plausibly subscribe. In the Dude's anti-establishment mentality, paraquat must have seemed comparable to the Agent Orange campaign to defoliate Vietnam. For the Dude, then, calling someone a human paraquat is the ultimate insult. Not only does the stuff destroy the source of other people's fun, it even poisons those who try to have a good time with whatever hasn't been killed off. Moreover, it represents the kind of 'scam' that would lead a 1960s throwback like the Dude to opt out of normal society. For the Dude, paraquat is the worst thing one can be, and the Big Lebowski is the ultimate buzz-kill, truly toxic to everything he touches, including those he is supposed to love most, his wife and his 'children'.

It is fair to say that we know more about what the Dude is against than what he is for, but he does have a kind of slacker philosophy, or at least an ethos. It is actually a worldview that seems similar to the Coens', as it has been expressed in a number of different films, and it is also linked to the religion of laughter promoted by Preston Sturges in *Sullivan's Travels*. The things that we ought to care about in life have been overlooked. We think we ought to care about money, status, success and all the other markers of how the world sorts out its winners and losers. But, in truth, everyone knows that these are not the things that really matter. Instead, we ought to enjoy the only life that has been given to us, with its simple pleasures of play, laughter, music, games and fellow-feeling. These things bring people together in *O Brother, Where Art Thou?*, while the grail quest for money and power breaks them apart. 'There's more to life than money, you know,' Marge Gunderson tells the killer she has apprehended at the end of *Fargo*. 'Don't you know that? And here ya are, and it's a beautiful day... Well, I just don't unnerstand it.' Similar notes are struck in *The Man Who Wasn't There*, in the music teacher's description of playing the piano with feeling rather than mere technical proficiency, a concept that Ed Crane simply cannot understand. Comically, and in a bitterly ironic move, he only loves dry cleaning, a completely chemical process that is not even tainted by water. Ed and his wife (to whom he does seem to bear some kind of attachment) loathe the Italian wedding they attend, with its pig-riding escapades and pie-eating contest, because they loathe life. *The Ladykillers*, like *O Brother*, suggests a contrasting redemption through joy in music, while *Fargo* offers even simpler pleasures, like Norm Gunderson's quest to get his nature painting on a US stamp. Alongside the battle between harmful and harmless idiots in the Coen oeuvre – a battle that comes to the fore at the climax of *Raising Arizona* and underpins all of *The Hudsucker Proxy* – is another, related theme, the battle between those who enjoy their life and those who don't.

Twenty-five dollars a day

In *Lebowski*, the bowling alley is obviously a location in which ordinary people get together for no other reason than to have a good time. It's impossible not to notice the camera's loving relationship to the place, its way of caressing surfaces and lingering on the craftsmanship that went into the 'Brunswick' style. Consider, above

Ed Crane, the man who wasn't there, unsmiling at a dance and uneasy around conspicuous joy

all, the shots from the opening credits, featuring all kinds of different people whose faces light up when their ball strikes the pins. Bowling is among the cheapest American fun to be had, where anyone at any level of skill can play without any degree of physical fitness or any of the typical trappings of 'jock' sports. Bowling is probably one of the least judgmental activities ever invented. At least for amateurs, it's more about having fun than keeping score. Walter's unhappiness and violent aggression is further emphasised, and undercut, by the absurdity of taking bowling so seriously, whereas the Dude's own relaxed attitude towards life is perfectly attuned to this particular pastime. He expressly tells the Big Lebowski that he won't allow his detective work to take precedence over bowling commitments – at once preposterously unprofessional and yet somehow just right. Bowling brings people together: it's the basis for an otherwise baffling friendship between a flaky ex-hippie peacenik and a bitterly unbalanced Vietnam vet, as well as the odd pairing between Jesus Quintana and Liam, his Irish bowling partner. It wouldn't be far-fetched to suggest that in *Lebowski* bowling seems to stand for the American dream of real friendship between people from different backgrounds and ethnicities, even if the point is disguised by absurdity. The bowling alley is a place where people can be themselves – among the film's most beautiful sequences is the one in which we simply watch folks bowl. This is the Dude's natural habitat. To nab a remark of the Stranger's, he fits right in there; so at home does he seem that we barely register the fact that he is never actually seen bowling.

The bowling alley is a people's palace, a place where all are welcome but in which the airs of the rich and ostentatious would seem out of place. No accident, then, that the Rolling Stones' 'Dead Flowers' (as covered by the brilliant Townes Van Zandt) accompanies the closing shots, with its acid contempt for someone 'sittin' there/In your silk upholstered chair/Talkin' to some rich folks that you know'. It is notable that the Dude's rejection of and disgust for the phoniness

and moral corruption of the upper crust is not based upon jealousy. Unimpressed by the Lebowski mansion, he tells Brandt that he might drop by again 'if I'm ever in the neighbourhood and I need to use the john'. As in so much Chandler, *Lebowski* is designed to meander through the castes and schedules of L.A., from the mean streets and dives to the money-drenched hills. The Coens are less insistent about the depravity of wealth than Chandler (or indeed the bitterly wrathful protagonist of *Cutter's Way*), but they do have a lead who simply isn't all that into cash.

The inadvertent heroism of the Dude's basic indifference to large sums of money is perhaps the one characteristic he actually has in common with Marlowe, who always insists on working only for his $25 a day plus expenses. This is not only a point of pride but a philosophy – albeit one unarticulated by the Dude – based upon the notion of avoiding the taint of the world. The classic hard-boiled

Heroic poses at the people's palace

Hollywood detective holds back not just from easy money but from compromising relationships as well, a fact that makes him an outsider in society. As Thomas Schatz notes, the 'isolated, self-reliant' private eye sets himself apart from the world out of 'deep-rooted idealism' that is only partially covered up by a cynical and jaded veneer of patter. 'The hardboiled detective's isolation, however,' writes Schatz, 'is not a function of intellect and breeding, but instead represents his outright rejection of a society whose values and attitudes he cannot accept or even understand.'[88] The Dude, as a 1960s throwback who still believes in 'opting out' of mainstream life, becomes a comic analogue, rather than an inversion, of the classic trope. Marlowe would be appalled by the Dude in many ways, one senses, but not by his attitude towards the Big Lebowski.

The Stranger's opening monologue describing the Dude, with its ironic reversal of the 'what's-a-hee-ro?' Hollywood concept of the hard-boiled detective as well as the typical protagonist of the Western, is actually what the film is about, just as Geoff Andrew suggests. The irony here, in other words, is designed to skewer generic conceptions and clichés, but not ultimately to encourage the audience to stop thinking about what heroism is, or to force the conclusion that heroism doesn't exist at all. As noted, the Coens' mode in *The Big Lebowski* links back to Hawks's mode in *The Big Sleep* not only as satirical subversion but also as genuine homage. 'Hawks is always looking at people, their gestures, their antics, their personality, with an eternally sad respect and fondness,' writes Thomson. *The Big Sleep* induces something very far from the noir style in which it is filmed, a giddiness, exuberance and delight that Thomson calls 'the pleasure, or the happiness or whatever you want to call it'.[89] The Coens are about the same work in *Lebowski*, particularly as their camera inhabits the bowling alley. The Coens mean *The Big Lebowski* to induce a similar response, some of that 'wonderful feeling' that Bob Dylan describes in 'The Man in Me', the soundtrack of the Dude's story.

The capacity for joy

The postmodern mode, however, with its hyper-allusive style and arch scepticism about the artificiality of narrative, often lacks a classically humane approach to character. The Coens, certainly in *Lebowski*, and in a number of their other films as well, seem to hark back to that humaneness in a way that many of their contemporaries do not. Tarantino actually retains a great deal of affection for many of his characters – consider John Travolta as the sad-sack, lovelorn assassin reading *Modesty Blaise* on the toilet just before he is gunned down, only to be 'resurrected' by *Pulp Fiction*'s circular structure – but mainly he is a brilliant impersonator of styles. The Coens are simply more expansive, and more capable of breaking through their own relentless irony. It would not be inaccurate to suggest that at their best they often 'work backwards' through satire and irony to a kind of heartfelt fondness for humanity with all its foibles, like Hawks, like Sturges and, in some ways, like Chandler.

Walter's cliff-side eulogy for Donny, given while holding his ashes in a coffee can, is a culminating moment in the film, an expression of what it is really about in many ways. The script, brilliantly played, improved and changed in a few subtle details in Goodman's extraordinary grandiloquent performance, reads:

Donny was a good bowler, and a good man. He was… He was one of us. He was a man who loved the outdoors, and bowling, and as a surfer explored the beaches of southern California from Redondo to Calabassos. And he was an avid bowler. And a good friend. He died – he died as so many of his generation, before his time. In your wisdom you took him, Lord. As you took so many bright flowering young men, at Khe San and Lan Doc and Hill 364. These young men gave their lives. And Donny too. Donny… who loved bowling –

Walter clears his throat.

…And so, Theodore – Donald – Kerabatsos, in accordance with what we think your dying wishes might well have been, we commit your mortal remains to the bosom of…

Walter is peeling the lid off the coffee can.

...the Pacific Ocean, which you loved so well...

As he shakes out the ashes.

...Goodnight, sweet prince...

The wind blows all of the ashes into the Dude, standing just to the side of and behind Walter.

One of the phrases absent from the scene in the actual film – about being a good friend – lies at the heart of this scene so clearly that it was probably deemed redundant to say it openly. Here is Walter: an outrageous and impossible buffoon whose ghastly and hilarious inappropriateness nevertheless manages to convey exactly how deeply and genuinely he loves his friend. His notion that Donny was 'a good bowler, and a good man' – in precisely that order – who 'loved the outdoors, and bowling' is priceless, calling to mind *Hamlet*'s gravediggers. And Walter's little quotation from *Hamlet* itself strikes exactly the right chord, simultaneously expressing both his grief and his foolishness. It's high dramatic irony: Walter means what he is saying literally and the audience is supposed to laugh at him good-naturedly behind his back; but we are also supposed to recognise his love for his friend, and therefore embrace him while we

The bereaved

are laughing – embrace him and forgive him for everything, just as the Dude does with a single hand gesture. The Dude is furious with the proceedings, but the scene ultimately ends with a hug between the two survivors that is actually very sweet. As Eddie Robson points out, Walter and the Dude are 'the bereaved'; Donny has no other family or friends and, in the final analysis, it turns out that they were the only people in the world who cared whether Donny lived or died.[90] These mortals may be fools, but they actually love each other. This makes them – and, arguably, the Coens – very different from the characters in and film-makers of the typical camp postmodern mode, which generally ends in cynicism and showy surface-effects rather than affirming life and ultimately choosing real feelings.

If there is a larger claim to be made about the importance of the Coens as film-makers, it involves this dimension of their films, of which *The Big Lebowski* is probably the finest example. All of the characteristic postmodern tricks are on display – the subversive mockery of narrative, the method of inhabiting a genre to expose its artificiality, the satirical thrust of its allusions to the classics, its disbelief in the old structures, tropes and systems – but they are not the ultimate purpose of the film. Irony, that slipperiest of all terms, is by no means being discarded by the Coens; if anything it is being amped up. But what might be called 'ironic effects' – verbal irony, dramatic irony and intertextual irony that brings in other works of art in order to tease them – are not the only effects that the Coens achieve. If there might be new horizons to be glimpsed beyond the postmodern, in which neither the old 'naively' realistic narratives, the experimental modernist techniques nor the postmodern recycling jobs reign supreme, the Coens seem like important precursors.

Despite their obvious and deliberate idiosyncrasy, the way in which the Coens seem to work 'backwards' through irony and cynicism to real emotional content resembles the style of the younger director Wes Anderson, whose films *Bottle Rocket, Rushmore* (1998), *The Royal Tenenbaums* (2001) and *The Life Aquatic with Steve Zissou* (2004) have a similarly humane approach to their obviously hopeless and sometimes deranged characters. The Coen style also bears comparison with the work of a crop of younger American male writers who came into prominence during the same cultural moment, like Dave Eggers and David Foster Wallace. In a 1993 interview, Wallace described what he was trying to do with his work, and aptly summarised an emerging *Zeitgeist* that could easily be applied to the Coens:

Fiction's about what it is to be a fucking *human being*... We've got all this 'literary' fiction that simply monotones that we're all becoming less and less human, that presents characters without souls or love... What's engaging and artistically real is, taking it as axiomatic that the present is grotesquely materialistic, how is it that we as human beings still have the capacity for joy, charity, genuine connections, for stuff that doesn't have a price?[91]

Down to the dodge of the expletive, which distinguishes them from the stuffiness of the 'square' realistic writers who preceded the high modernists and postmodernists, these writers are of the Coens' ilk, they inhabit a similar time and place, and they are addressing some of the same issues. In his memoir *A Heartbreaking Work of Staggering Genius* (2000) – a title that has the same mock-serious ring to it as *O Brother, Where Art Thou?* – Eggers asked, at once joking and in earnest, what sort of emotional content you could bring to phrases like 'Dude, she died'. If anything, 'the Dude abides' has the opposite valence, but a similar idea lies behind it. The phrase is a silly but harmless and somewhat self-mocking expression of a hedonistic worldview that rejects the cares of a mad, mad, mad, mad world in favour of simple pleasures – the holy fool 'taking it easy for all us sinners', as the Stranger puts it.

Simultaneously, the phrase comically blasphemes the Lord God, who is well known to advertise Himself as the only being that abides forever. The rest of us pass away 'like grass', as the quotation from the Bible reads behind the undertaker at the mortuary; or a tumbleweed. The Dude claims that he abides, but maybe he means to say that he is well aware that he only abides for a while. In that case, his argument seems to run – and in essence this is the argument of the film – why get yourself all twisted up in knots trying to scramble for money, status, fame, power and so forth? Why not enjoy yourself, why not enjoy your life, since it's the only one you have anyway? I mean it, the film seems to say, and this time I mean it honestly: fuck it, let's go bowling.

Notes

1 The web portal for all this madness, as well as our source here, is http://www.lebowskifest.com. The Links section leads to a plethora of news reports, fan sites and trivia pages with more information and wacky loving attention than can be described here.

2 A list of papers delivered at the symposium, which was convened by two professors of English literature, Aaron Jaffe and Ed Comentale, can be found online at The Lebowski Cult, An Academic Symposium (http://www.louisville.edu/a-s/cchs/lebowski/papers.html). The content of these papers was unavailable to the authors at the time of writing, but in their online 'Letter to Donny' the organisers suggest that 'any difference between fans and scholars is strictly academic'.

3 See http://www.bluerat.com/llua/index.html.

4 David Edelstein, 'You're Entering a World of Lebowski', *The New York Times*, 8 August 2004.

5 Ethan Coen and Joel Coen, *The Big Lebowski* (Faber, 1998), p. vii. All references to the script are taken from this edition. Where the film differs from the script we favour the film, unless otherwise stated.

6 William Preston Robertson, *The Big Lebowski: The Making of a Coen Brothers Film*, ed. Tricia Cooke (Norton, 1998). Robertson's text was edited by Tricia Cooke, Ethan Coen's wife, who is a credited co-editor on recent Coen films, including *Lebowski*, a fact which reinforces the book's credibility while at the same time suggesting the film-makers' longstanding desire to control their self-presentation. Because so much inaccurate information about the Coens is floating around, we will generally source Robertson for reliable production information about the film.

7 The former was Quentin Curtis of the *Daily Telegraph*, the latter Matthew Sweet of *The Independent*.

8 Robertson, *The Big Lebowski*, p. 45.

9 These are: '(1) howling fat men, (2) blustery titans, (3) vomiting, (4) violence, (5) dreams, and (6) peculiar haircuts.' Robertson, *The Big Lebowski*, p. 16.

10 Richard Schickel, *Double Indemnity* (BFI, 1992), p. 21.

11 Robertson, *The Big Lebowski*, p. 78.

12 Michel Ciment and Hubert Niogret, 'The Logic of Soft Drugs', in Paul A. Woods (ed.), *Joel and Ethan Coen, Blood Siblings* (Plexus, 2003), p. 168.

13 For an exhaustive rundown of the film's locations, see http://www.geocities.com/locationfreak/ftd.html.

14 Ciment and Niogret, 'The Logic of Soft Drugs', p. 168.

15 Schickel, *Double Indemnity*, p. 10.

16 Robertson, *The Big Lebowski*, p. 130.

17 Making of documentary on *The Big Lebowski* DVD; see also Eddie Robson, *Coen Brothers* (Virgin Film, 2003), p. 175.

18 Robertson, *The Big Lebowski*, p. 38.

19 Ibid., p. 39.

20 Bill Green, Ben Peskoe, Will Russell and Scott Shuffitt, *I'm A Lebowski, You're A Lebowski: The Ultimate Guide to the Coen Brothers' Cult Classic Film* (Canongate, 2007). This marvellous book also includes interviews with Dowd, Milius, Freeman and Abernathy, who also recalls being called to a mansion and ushered into a room to find a nude, paint-covered female artist 'on a bungee cord making body prints on the floor'; a Malibu cop bouncing a coffee cup off his head and telling him to 'stay out of my beach community'; and cremated remains being blown back onto mourners when scattered from a clifftop.

21 Andy Lowe, 'The Brothers Grim', in Woods, *Joel and Ethan Coen*, p. 163.

22 Robertson, *The Big Lebowski*, p. 41.

23 David Thomson, *The Big Sleep* (BFI, 1997), p. 13.

24 Robson, *Coen Brothers*, p. 182.

25 Ciment and Niogret, 'The Logic of Soft Drugs', p. 173.

26 They really hit it big the next year with 'Ruby, Don't Take Your Love to Town', a song that might have struck a chord with Walter or the Big Lebowski. It concerns an embittered, disabled Korean War veteran who reminds his heartless young lover that 'It wasn't me that started that old crazy Asian war/But I was proud to go and do my patriotic chore', while also acknowledging that 'It's hard to love a man whose legs are bent and paralysed/And the wants and the needs of a woman of your age, Ruby, I realise'.

27 According to the Coens on the making-of featurette on *The Big Lebowski* DVD, producer Joel Silver suggested that some kind of climactic rug restoration might have provided a satisfying pay-off; tied the picture together, if you like.

28 See http://www.familymediaguide. com/media/onDVD/media-433568. html.

29 Ciment and Niogret, 'The Logic of Soft Drugs', p. 170.

30 Lowe, 'The Brothers Grim', p. 163. Ethan cites Barton Fink's relationship with Charlie Meadows, also played by Goodman, as a precedent.

31 *Crimewave* (1985, written by the Coens and directed by Sam Raimi) would make seven, but *Crimewave* doesn't count.

32 Ethan Coen, *Gates of Eden* (Weisbach Morrow, 1998), p. 69. Other stories feature characters such as Victor Strang, a useless private eye who gets his ear bitten off and spat ten feet in the air, and Joe Carmody, who blunders his way around in the boxing underworld.

33 See Kristin Thompson and David Bordwell, *Film History: An Introduction* (2nd edn, McGraw-Hill, 2002), p. 698. 'Genre conventions could be inflated or deflated,' Thompson and Bordwell note of the Coens, outlining the influence of Sturges and Capra on their work.

34 Stephen Hunter, 'Kill Me Again: The Rise of Nouveau Noir', in Ed Gorman, Martin H. Greenberg and Lee Server (eds), *The Big Book of Noir* (Carroll and Graf, 1998), p. 143.

35 Raymond Borde and Étienne Chaumeton, *A Panorama of American Film Noir 1941–1953*, trans. Paul Hammond (City Lights, 2002), p. 122.

36 Pauline Kael, 'Blood Simple' (review), *The New Yorker*, 25 February 1985.

37 Bob Strauss, 'Film Noir Seduces the '90s', *Boston Sunday Globe*, 23 April 1995.

38 Raymond Chandler quote and list of Chandler-related noir in Thomas Schatz, *Hollywood Genres: Formulas, Filmmaking, and the Studio System* (McGraw-Hill, 1981), p. 126.

39 Robertson, *The Big Lebowski*, p. 51.

40 Ibid., p. 43.

41 Raymond Chandler, 'The Simple Art of Murder', in Chandler, *Later Novels & Other Writings* (Library of America, 1995), pp. 991–2.

42 Lowe; 'The Brothers Grim', p. 163.

43 Ciment and Niogret, 'The Logic of Soft Drugs', p. 167.

44 Robertson, *The Big Lebowski*, p. 42.

45 Lowe, 'The Brothers Grim', p. 163.

46 Ciment and Niogret, 'The Logic of Soft Drugs', p. 167.

47 On this process, and the film, see Thomson, *The Big Sleep*.

48 Raymond Chandler, *Stories & Early Novels* (Library of America, 1995), p. 888; the angular building appears on p. 874. Another instance of borrowing involves a piece of dialogue in the screenplay that was cut from the film. When the Dude is being interviewed by the police about his stolen car, one of the cops tells him, 'Me, I don't drink coffee. But it's nice when they offer.' In Chandler's *The High Window*, Marlowe thinks to himself, 'I don't like port in hot weather, but it's nice when they let you refuse it.' See Coen and Coen, *The Big Lebowski*, p. 57, and Chandler, *Stories & Early Novels*, p. 992.

49 Chandler, *Stories & Early Novels*, pp. 993–4.

50 On Hawks's *modus operandi*, see Thomson, *The Big Sleep*, p. 34. On the Coens' storyboarding obsession and its effect on almost every dimension of their films, see Robertson, *The Big Lebowski*, pp. 53–66. *Lebowski* contains slightly more improvisation than most of their films. Eddie Robson is wrong in asserting that the Dude's summary judgment of the Big Lebowski as a 'human paraquat' isn't in the script, but the filmed scene does deviate notably from the written text. See Robson, *Coen Brothers*, p. 186; cf. Coen and Coen, *The Big Lebowski*, pp. 121–4.

51 Robertson, *The Big Lebowski*, p. 127.

52 Ibid., pp. 100–2. The restaurants in the film are apparently Johnnie's on Fairfax and Wiltshire, and Dinah's in Culver City. See Robson, *Coen Brothers*, p. 179. The bowling alley, Hollywood Star Lanes, has now closed. For a virtual tour of the real locations used in the film, see 'Follow the Dude' at http://www.geocities.com/locationfreak /ftd.html.

53 Robertson, *The Big Lebowski*, pp. 116–17.

54 Thomson, *The Big Sleep*, p. 51.

55 See Robson, *Coen Brothers*, p. 190.

56 Raymond Chandler, letter to D. J. Ibberson, 19 April 1951, in *Later Novels & Other Writings*, p. 1044.

57 Thomson, *The Big Sleep*, p. 67. For the previous quotations, see pp. 10, 39 and 42.

58 Chandler, *Stories & Early Novels*, p. 730.

59 Thomson, *The Big Sleep*, p. 64.

60 See Thomson, *The Big Sleep*, p. 21.

61 On masculinity and 'matrophobia' in early twentieth-century literature and culture, see Ann Douglas, *Terrible Honesty: Mongrel Manhattan in the 1920s* (FSG Noonday, 1995), p. 8.

62 Bonus feature *Miller's Crossing* DVD.

63 David Thomson, *The New Biographical Dictionary of Film* (New York: Knopf, 2002), p. 174.

64 Cormac McCarthy, *No Country for Old Men* (Picador, 2005), p. 279.

65 Robson, *Coen Brothers*, p. 191.

66 Robertson, *The Big Lebowski*, p. 146.

67 Quintana's outburst could be compared to an exchange from 'Destiny', the first story in *Gates of Eden*, which concludes with a duff boxer turned duff private eye meeting with a man whom he has photographed having sex with his client's wife:

'You see, dontcha, what's goin on between me and Benny Benedeck?'

He took another puff on his cigar then stared at it once again.

'Well,' I cleared my throat. 'Well, sir, it seems as if each of you is trying to establish dominance.'

'Dominance?' This brought his eyes up from the cigar.

'Well, yes sir, through sexual, uh – Well, it's not uncommon in the animal kingdom – Not that either party here is, uh – But, you know, territorial marking, and the, er, the female … Uh, well, the male display, and, uh …'

'Dominance.' He looked back at the cigar. After a musing silence he cleared his throat.

'That sex act, you know, which you witnessed between myself and Mrs Benedeck. You may have noticed I yelled the name "Benny Benedeck." Many times I called his name.' He lapsed into silence.

'Yes, sir,' I said.

'In yelling his name, does this mean I fantasise' – he waved his hands in a dreamy gesture – 'about sex with Benny Benedeck? That I fuck mentally him? Does this mean that I am a fruit?' He gravely shook his head. 'No, for I am not a fruit. No, what you have here, in this sex act, I piss in Benny Benedeck's ear.' (Coen, *Gates of Eden*, p. 24.)

68 It is interesting to note that while shooting the film, the Coens were doing their best to navigate the undesired brouhaha of *Fargo*'s Oscar nominations. In a suitably Dude-like fashion, they've done their best to shrug off fame and 'achievement'. In an article about his time working as a junior assistant on the film, Alex Belth reports 'the boys' unwillingness to play party to any of the hype'. See 'Strikes and Gutters: A Year with the Coen Brothers', http://www.youknow-forkids.com/yearwithcoens.htm. An earlier version of the article is also included in *Projections 8* (Faber, 1998).

69 Robertson, *The Big Lebowski*, p. 126.

70 Ibid., p. 57.

71 'Being True to the Character: Frances McDormand Talks to Willem Dafoe', in John Boorman and Walter Donahue (eds), *The Director's Cut: The Best of Projections*, John Boorman and Walter Donahue (eds) (Faber, 2006), p. 141. Article originally published in *Projections 7*, (Faber, 1997).

72 Another would be the discovery of the theft of the Dude's car from the bowling alley car lot.

73 See Ron Rosenbaum, 'Dude, Where's My Dude?', *New York Observer*, 7 July 2003.

74 Scott F. Kiesling, 'Dude', *American Speech*, vol. 9 no. 3, Autumn 2004, pp. 281–305, also available online at http://www.pitt.edu/~kiesling/dude/dude.pdf.

75 Robson, *Coen Brothers*, p. 166.

76 For these quotations, more on the film's reception and box-office figures, see ibid., pp. 182–5, an excellent summary we follow here.

77 Curtis and Sweet, for example, both already quoted in the Introduction.

78 Geoff Andrew, 'The Big Lebowski' (review), *Time Out*, 22 April 1998.

79 Geoff Andrew, *Stranger Than Paradise: Maverick Film-makers in Recent American Cinema* (Prion, 1998). Andrew also draws attention to the film's probing of masculinity and the Dude's essential decency.

80 On the Coens' use of Shakespeare and other literary references, see Morgan Meis and J. M. Tyree, 'Is It OK to Read the Coen Brothers as Literature?', *Gettysburg Review*, Spring 2006.

81 Robertson, *The Big Lebowski*, p. 99.

82 Barton Fink, with his pompous dreams of a 'new theatre' for 'the common man', would have approved; Fink is a Sullivan analogue of sorts in that he learns a lesson about his pretensions, although his suffering at the hands of his neighbour is more strange, intense and hallucinatory.

83 In his account of his time as a junior assistant on the film, Alex Belth reported a comparable tenor to the way the Coens broke the news that, due to an injury, Belth was to be removed from the shoot. 'Joel put his arm around me in a rare moment of physical affection and then slowly started to laugh reflexively. "We feel really horrible." "I'm fucking fucked, right?" Ethan, peaking up, started to laugh too. Grief support in its purest form.' See http://www.youknow-forkids.com/yearwithcoens.htm.

84 Robertson, *The Big Lebowski*, pp. 20–1.

85 Robson, *Coen Brothers*, p. 191.

86 While the Dude might not bother to open the briefcase, would Walter really not want to have a look? The plot requires them not to notice that the briefcase has no money in it.

87 Thanks to Geoff Andrew for the observation that the Dude's attitude to sex is much like his attitude to money: 'he is not predatory, hardly adept at flirting, unbothered to some extent by Quintana's sexuality – he has a use for sex, but little obvious *desire*. He has more time for affection than lust or longing, it seems.'

88 Thomas Schatz, *Hollywood Genres: Formulas, Filmmaking, and the Studio System* (McGraw-Hill, 1981), p. 125.

89 Thomson, *The Big Sleep*, p. 10.

90 Robson, *Coen Brothers*, p. 188.

91 Larry McCaffrey, 'An Interview with David Foster Wallace', *The Review of Contemporary Fiction*, Summer 1993, pp. 131–2.

Credits

The Big Lebowski
USA/Great Britain 1998

Directed by
Joel Coen
Produced by
Ethan Coen
Written by
Ethan Coen
and Joel Coen
Director of Photography
Roger Deakins A.S.C.,
B.S.C.
Edited by
Roderick Jaynes
[i.e. Joel & Ethan Coen]
and Tricia Cooke
Production Designer
Rick Heinrichs
Original Music by
Carter Burwell

©1998. PolyGram Filmed
Entertainment, Inc.
Production Companies
PolyGram Filmed
Entertainment presents
a Working Title
production

Executive Producers
Tim Bevan
Eric Fellner
Co-producer
John Cameron
**Unit Production
Manager**
John Cameron

Production Supervisor
Gilly Ruben
Production Coordinator
Gregg Edler
**Assistant Production
Coordinator**
Tom Elkins
**Set Production
Assistants**
Rita Lisa Danao
Randol P. Taylor
Tammy Dickson
**Assistant to Mr.
Goodman**
Patricia Douglas
Assistant to Mr. Bevan
Juliette Dow
Assistants to Mr. Fellner
Amelia Granger
Lara Thompson
Production Interns
Stacy Minkowsky
Lauren Lapham
Location Manager
Robert Graf
**Assistant Location
Manager**
Kim Jordan
Location Assistants
Chris Fuentes
Valerie Jo Burnley
**Post Production
Supervisor**
Charlie Vogel
**Post Production
Facilities**
C5
Sound One Corporation
**Executive in Charge of
Production**
Jane Frazer

**President of Operations
for Mike Zoss
Productions**
Alan J. Schoolcraft
Accountant
Mindy Sheldon
Assistant Accountant
Kris Soderquist
Payroll Accountant
Jery Legget
**Accounting Production
Assistant**
Aillene Laure Bubis
Production Secretary
Kimberly Rach
Company Coordinator
Nina Khoshaba
Office Assistant
Marty Houston
First Assistant Director
Jeff Rafner
**Key Second Assistant
Director**
Conte Mark Matal
**Second Second
Assistant Director**
Donald Murphy
Script Supervisor
T. Kukowinski
Casting by
John Lyons C.S.A.
Casting Associate
Wendy Weidman
Casting Assistant
Jenna Dupree
**Extras Casting
Coordinator**
Cecily Jordan

Extras Casting Assistant
Fonda Anita
Camera Operator
Ted Morris
First Assistant Camera
Andy Harris
Second Assistant Camera
Adam Gilmore
Camera Loader
Ed Dally
Aerial Cameraman
Ron Goodman
Aerial Camera Assistants
Dave Sale
Jeremy Braben
Chief Lighting Technician
Bill O'Leary
Assistant Chief Lighting Technicians
Alan P. Colbert
Alan Frazier
Electricians
Roman Jakobi
Jon Salzman
Duncan M. Sobel
Abbe Wool
Rigger Gaffer
Marty Bosworth
Rigging Best Boy Electric
Chris Reddish
Rigging Electricians
Craig A. Brink
David Diamond
Jimmy Ellis
Jenifer Galvez
Kevin Brown

First Company Grip
Les Percy
Second Company Grip
Wayne Kosky
Dolly Grip
Bruce Hamme
Grips
Charlie Edwards
Tony Boura
Charles Smith
Key Rigging Grip
Jerry Day
Rigging Best Boy Grip
Bill Green
Rigging Grips
Alvaro Martinez
Phil Aubry
Michael Stringer
Robert King
Video Assist
Marty Weight
Still Photographer
Merrick Morton
Visual Effects Supervisor
Janek Sirrs
Visual Effects by
The Computer Film Company, Inc.
Visual Effects Producer
Janet Yale
Compositing Artists
David Fuhrer
Travis Bauman
Donovan Scott
3D Artist
Robert Chapin

Paint Artists
Katie Hecker
Susan Evans
Matt Dessero
Mechanical Effects Designer
Peter Chesney
Special Effects Foremen
Tom Chesney
Mick Duff
Effects Technicians
Chris Nelson
Barry Beaulac
Big Associate Editor
Big Dave Diliberto
Assistant Editors
Liza Mozden
Alex Belth
Apprentice Editor
Karyn Anonia
Art Director
John Dexter
Set Decorator
Chris Spellman
Storyboard Artist
J. Todd Anderson
Set Designer
Mariko Braswell
Graphic Designer
Bradford Richardson
Art Department Coordinator
Lori Ashcraft
Leadperson
Tim Snowber
Co-leadperson
Karen Agresti
On-set Dresser
Lisa A. Corbin

Set Dressers
Beth Emerson
Tim Park
Art Department Assistant
Sydney Ann Lunn
Property Master
Ritchie Kremer
Assistant Property Master
Ron Patterson
Property Handler
Carolyn Lassek
Propmaker Foremen
David Boucher
Franklin P. Healy
Propmaker Gang Bosses
Douglas Dewaay
Mark Haber
Aaron Harney
Brett Hernandez
Steven D. Powell
Construction Coordinator
Tim Lafferty
Construction Estimator
Kathleen Walker
Labourer Foreman
Charles Reyes
Labourer Gang Boss
Phillip Vargas
Tool Man
Larry Wise
Head Painter
Anthony Gaudio
Stand-by Painter
John Railton
Painter Foremen
Wayne Nycz
Gary Osborn

Greensman
Philip C. Hurst
Costume Designer
Mary Zophres
Assistant Costume Designer
Sonya Ooten
Costume Supervisor
Pam Withers
Key Set Costumer
Cookie Lopez
Set Costumer
Virginia Seffens-Burton
Make-up Supervisor
Jean Black
Make-up for Mr. Bridges
Edouard Henriques
Hair Stylist
Daniel Curet
Title Sequence and 'Gutterballs' Titles Designed and Produced by
Balsmeyer & Everett, Inc.
Designer
Randall Balsmeyer
Animation Producer
Kathy Kelehan
Computer Animators
Daniel Leung
Amit Sethi
Matt McDonald
Gray Miller
Opticals by
John Alagna
(The Effects House)
János Pilenyi
(Cineric Inc.)
Colour Timer
David Orr

Negative Cutter
Mo Henry
Original Music Orchestrated by
Carter Burwell
Sonny Kompanek
Music Engineer
Michael Farrow
Music Supervisor
Happy Walters
Executive in Charge of Music for PolyGram Filmed Entertainment
Dawn Solér
Senior VP for PolyGram Soundtracks
Jacquie Perryman
Music Coordinators
Spring Aspers
Manish Raval
Tom Wolfe
Musical Archivist
T-Bone Burnett
Music Contractor
Emile Charlap
Recorded at
Right Track Recording
(New York City)
Music Editor
Todd Kasow
Associate Music Editor
Missy Cohen
Music Playback
Brian McCarty
Soundtrack
"The Man in Me" written and performed by Bob Dylan; "Ataypura" written by Moises Vivancco, performed by

Yma Sumac; "Behave Yourself" written by Booker T. Jones, Steve Cropper, Al Jackson, Jr., Lewie Steinberg, performed by Booker T. & the MG's; 'Branded' theme song written by Alan Alch, Dominic Frontiere; "Dead Flowers" written by Mick Jagger, Keith Richards, performed by Townes Van Zandt; "Glück das mir verlieb" from the opera *Die tote Stadt* written and conducted by Erich Wolfgang Korngold, performed by Ilona Steingruber, Anton Dermota and the Austrian State Radio Orchestra; "Her Eyes Are a Blue Million Miles" written by Don Vliet, performed by Captain Beefheart; "Hotel California" written by Don Henley, Glenn Frey, Don Felder, performed by the Gipsy Kings; "I Got It Bad & That Ain't Good" written by Duke Ellington, Paul Francis Webster, performed by Nina Simone; "I Hate You" written by Gary Burger, David Havlicek, Roger Johnston, Thomas

E. Shaw, Larry Spangler, performed by Monks; "Just Dropped In (To See What Condition My Condition Was In)" written by Mickey Newbury, performed by Kenny Rogers & the New Edition; "Mucha Muchacha" written by Juan Garcia Esquivel, performed by Esquivel; "My Mood Swings" written by Elvis Costello, Cait O'Riordan, performed by Elvis Costello; "Oye como va" written by Tito Puente, performed by Santana; "Pictures at an Exhibition" written by Modest Mussorgsky, performed by the Royal Concertgebouw Orchestra, conducted by Sir Colin Davis; "Requiem in D Minor" written by W. A. Mozart, performed by the Slovak Philharmonic Orchestra and Choir; "Run through the Jungle" written by John Fogerty, performed by Creedence Clearwater Revival; "Stamping Ground" written by Louis Hardin (a.k.a. Moondog), performed by Moondog with Orchestra; "Standing on the Corner"

written by Frank Loesser, performed by Dean Martin; "Tammy" written by Ray Evans, Jay Livingston, performed by Debbie Reynolds; "Traffic Boom" written and performed by Piero Piccioni; "Tumbling Tumbleweeds" written by Bob Nolan, performed by the Sons of the Pioneers; "Viva Las Vegas" written by Doc Pomus, Mort Shuman, performed by Shawn Colvin, "Viva Las Vegas" also performed by Big Johnson; "Walking Song" written and performed by Meredith Monk; "We Venerate Thy Cross" performed by the Rustavi Choir.

Soundtrack Available on
Mercury Records (a PolyGram Company)
Choreographers
Bill and Jacqui Landrum
Sound Mixer
Allan Byer
Boom Operators
Keenan Wyatt
Peter Kurland
Utility Sound Technician
Sam Sarkar
Re-recording Mixers
Michael Barry
Skip Lievsay

Supervising Sound Editor
Skip Lievsay
Dialogue Editors
Magdaline Volaitis
Rick Freeman
FX Editor
Lewis Goldstein
Assistant Sound Editors
Kimberly McCord
Wyatt Sprague
Transfer Assistant Editor
Anne Pope
Apprentice Sound Editor
Allan Zaleski
Intern Sound Editor
Igor Nicholich
ADR Editor
Kenton Jakub
Foley Supervisor
Ben Cheah
Foley Artist
Marko Costanzo
Foley Mixer
Bruce Pross
Foley Editors
Jennifer Ralston
Frank Kern
Dolby Consultant
Bradford Hohle
Stunt Coordinator
Jery Hewitt
Stunts
Jennifer Lamb
Vince Deadrick Jr.
Loyd Catlett

Stand-ins
Ken Kells
Frank Turner
Transportation Coordinator
Don Tardino
Transportation Captains
Thomas Vilardo
Tim Ryan
Transportation Estimator
Derek Wade
Production Van Drivers
Michael E. Cain
Anthony K. Riedel
Honeywagon Driver
Denis Junt
Catering
Entertainment Motion
Picture Catering
Clement Bacque
Eric Vignando
Crafts Service
Gary Kramer
Production Goddess
Karyn Anonia
Left Behind
Margaret Hayes
Bowling Pro
Barry Asher
First Aid
Thomas W. Foster
Jonas C. Matz
Legal Services
Shays & Murphy
Financial Consultant
Rashid Chinchanwala
Legal Advisers
Angela Morrison
Rachel Holroyd

Dialect Coach
Liz Himelstein
Animals
Animal Actors
Baby Wranglers
Patti Cooke
Eileen Sullivan
Giggles/Howls/Marmots
William Preston
Robertson
Publicist
Larry Kaplan
Special Thanks
Clay Rand; Cinema
Vehicle Services;
Hollywood Star Lanes;
AMSPEC; Brian Biles;
Emil Moscowitz; Patrick
Sheedy; Gary Spero; Liz
Young; Señor Greaser
Stock Footage
CNN
Blue Sky Stock Footage
Lighting & Grip Equipment Supplied by
Paskal Lighting
Arriflex 535 Cameras by
Otto Nemenz
Aerial Camera Equipment Supplied by
Spacecam System, Inc.

CAST
Jeff Bridges
Jeffrey Lebowski,
'The Dude'
John Goodman
Walter Sobchak
Julianne Moore
Maude Lebowski
Steve Buscemi
Theodore Donald
'Donny' Kerabatsos
Peter Stormare
Uli Kunkel, nihilist
David Huddleston
Jeffrey Lebowski,
'The Big Lebowski'
**Philip Seymour
Hoffman**
Brandt
Flea
Kieffer, nihilist
Leon Russom
Malibu police chief
and **Sam Elliott**
as the Stranger
with **John Turturro**
as Jesus Quintana
Ben Gazzara
as Jackie Treehorn
David Thewlis
as Knox Harrington
Tara Reid
Bunny Lebowski
Philip Moon
Treehorn thug
Mark Pellegrino
Treehorn thug
Torsten Voges
Franz, nihilist

Jimmie Dale Gilmore
Smokey
Jack Kehler
Marty, The Dude's
landlord
James G. Hoosier
Liam O'Brien, Quintana's
partner
Carlos Leon
Maude's thug #1
Terrance Burton
Maude's thug #2
Richard Gant
older cop
Christian Clemenson
younger cop
Dom Irrera
Tony the chauffeur
Gérard L'Heureux
Lebowski's chauffeur
Lu Elrod
coffee shop waitress
Michael Gomez
auto circus cop
Peter Siragusa
Gary the bartender
Marshall Manesh
doctor
Harry Bugin
Arthur Digby Sellers
Jesse Flanagan
Little Larry Sellers
Irene Olga López
Pilar, Sellers'
housekeeper
Luis Colina
Corvette owner
Ajgie Kirkland
cab driver

Jon Polito
Da Fino, private snoop
Aimee Mann
nihilist woman
Jerry Haleva
Saddam
Jennifer Lamb
pancake waitress
Warren David Keith
Francis Donnelly, funeral
director
Holly Copeland
Karen Christenberry
Natalie Webb
Julie Bond
Kim Yates
Elizabeth A. Eaton
Lori Jo Birdsell
Kelly Sheerin
Kiva Dawson
Lisa C. Boltauzer
Alison Simpson
Lindsay Fellenbaum
Melissa Aggeles
Katherine Slay
Jennifer S. Garett
Danielle Nicole Parish
Jennifer Strovas
Jamie Green
Caitlin McLean
Michelle E. Swanson
Laurel Kitten
Joelle Martinec
Amy Tinkham
Mary Lee
Sandra Plazinic
Bree Turner
Carrie Macy
Jacqui Landrum
Martina Volpp

**Danielle Marcus
Janssen
Wendy Braun
Amy Warren
Michelle Rudy-
Mirkovich**
dancers

Dolby Digital/DTS/SDDS
Colour by
Technicolor
Produced on
Kodak film
MPAA no.
**35633
IATSE**

Released in the US by
Gramercy Pictures on 6
March 1998, MPAA rating
R, at circa 117 minutes
Released in the UK by
PolyGram Film
Distributors on 1 May
1998, BBFC certificate
18 (no cuts), at 116
minutes 53 seconds

Filmed from 27 January
1997 to 24 April 1997 on
location in California
(USA). Budget reported
as $15 million

Credits compiled by
Julian Grainger

Bibliography

Books and articles

Andrew, Geoff, 'The Big Lebowski' (review), *Time Out*, 22 April 1998.

Andrew, Geoff, *Stranger Than Paradise: Maverick Film-makers in Recent American Cinema* (London: Prion, 1998).

Borde, Raymond and Etienne Chaumeton, *A Panorama of American Film Noir 1941–1953*, trans. Paul Hammond (San Francisco: City Lights, 2002).

Chandler, Raymond, *Later Novels & Other Writings, Stories & Early Novels* (New York: Library of America, 1995).

———, *Stories & Early Novels* (New York: Library of America, 1995).

Ciment, Michel and Hubert Niogret, 'The Logic of Soft Drugs', in Paul A. Woods (ed.), *Joel and Ethan Coen, Blood Siblings* (London: Plexus, 2003).

Coen, Ethan, *Gates of Eden* (New York: Weisbach Morrow, 1998).

———, *Blood Simple* (New York: St Martin's, 1988).

———, *Barton Fink/Miller's Crossing* (Boston/London: Faber, 1991).

———, *Fargo* (London: Faber, 1996).

———, *The Big Lebowski* (London: Faber, 1998).

———, *The Man Who Wasn't There* (London: Faber, 2001).

Dafoe, Willem, and Frances McDormand, 'Being True to the Character: Frances McDormand talks to Willem Dafoe', in *Projections The Director's Cut (The Best of 14 Years)*, John Boorman and Walter Donahue, eds (London: Faber, 2006), pp. 126–44. Interview first published in Boorman and Donahue (eds), *Projections 7* (London: Faber, 1997).

Douglas, Ann, *Terrible Honesty: Mongrel Manhattan in the 1920s* (New York: FSG/Noonday, 1995)

Edelstein, David, 'You're Entering a World of Lebowski', *The New York Times*, 8 August 2004.

Green, Bill, Ben Peskoe, Will Russell and Scott Shuffitt, *I'm A Lebowski, You're A Lebowski: The Ultimate Guide to the Coen Brothers' Cult Classic Film* (Edinburgh: Canongate, 2007).

Hunter, Stephen, 'Kill Me Again: The Rise of Nouveau Noir', in Ed Gorman, Martin H. Greenberg and Lee Server (eds), *The Big Book of Noir* (New York: Carroll and Graf, 1998).

Kael, Pauline, 'Blood Simple' (review), *The New Yorker*, 25 February 1985.

Kiesling, Scott F., 'Dude', *American Speech* vol. 79 no. 3, Autumn 2004.

Lowe, Andy, 'The Brothers Grim', in Paul A. Woods (ed.), *Joel and Ethan Coen, Blood Siblings* (London: Plexus, 2003).

McCaffrey, Larry, 'An Interview with David Foster Wallace', *The Review of Contemporary Fiction*, Summer 1993.

McCarthy, Cormac, *No Country for Old Men* (London: Picador, 2005).

Meis, Morgan and J. M. Tyree, 'Is It OK to Read the Coen Brothers as Literature?', *Gettysburg Review*, Spring 2006.

Robertson, William Preston, *The Big Lebowski: The Making of a Coen Brothers Film*, ed. Tricia Cooke (New York: Norton, 1998).

Robson, Eddie, *Coen Brothers* (London: Virgin Film, 2003).

Rosenbaum, Ron, 'Dude, Where's My Dude?: Dudelicious Dissection, From Sontag to Spicoli', *New York Observer*, 7 July 2003.

Schatz, Thomas, *Hollywood Genres: Formulas, Filmmaking, and the Studio System* (New York: McGraw-Hill, 1981).

Schickel, Richard, *Double Indemnity* (London: BFI, 1992).

Strauss, Bob, 'Film Noir Seduces the '90s', *Boston Sunday Globe*, 23 April 1995.

Thompson, Kristin and David Bordwell, *Film History: An Introduction*, 2nd edn (New York: McGraw-Hill, 2002).

Thomson, David, *The Big Sleep* (London: BFI, 1997).

——, *The New Biographical Dictionary of Film* (New York: Knopf, 2002).

Woods, Paul A. (ed.), *Joel and Ethan Coen, Blood Siblings* (London: Plexus, 2003).

Online sources

The Big Lebowski: IMDb's Complete Soundtrack, Cast, Crew, Credits and Trivia
<www.imdb.com/title/tt0118715>

Lebowski Fest Home Page and Web Portal
<www.lebowskifest.com>

The Lebowski Cult: An Academic Symposium (September, 2006)
<www.louisville.edu/a-s/cchs/lebowski> (NB. This site lists paper titles, but content is unavailable)

'Follow the Dude' Lebowski Locations
<www.geocities.com/locationfreak/ftd.html>

Family Media Guide on *The Big Lebowski*
<www.familymediaguide.com/media/onDVD/media-433568.html>

Little Lebowski Urban Achievers' 'Official' Website
<www.bluerat.com/llua>

Alex Belth: 'Strikes and Gutters: A Year with the Coen Brothers'
<www.youknow-forkids.com/yearwithcoens.htm>

Dudeism – The Church of the Latter-Day Dude
<www.dudeism.com>

Note: much of the material from the Lebowski Cult Symposium, 'Follow the Dude' location site and Dudeism site is reprinted in *I'm A Lebowski, You're A Lebowski* (Green et al., see Bibliography).